CONFECTIONS

DÉLICES CRÉOLES

CONFECTIONS

EXOTIC DESSERTS FROM THE FRENCH CARIBBEAN

KÖNEMANN

Acknowledgments

Level of difficulty of the recipes:

✱   easy
✱✱   advanced
✱✱✱   challenging

Original edition 1997 © Fabien Bellahsen und Daniel Rouche
Photos: Studio Lucien Loeb/Didier Bizos
Original title: Délices des Îles - Confitures, Chocolats, Viennoiseries

Recipe Coordinator:
Jean Bordier
Meilleur ouvrier de France, Président d'Honneur de l'Association des Maîtres Cuisiniers de France, Membre titulaire de l'Académie Culinaire de France, Chevalier de l'Ordre National du Mérite, Officier du Mérite agricole

Chefs and Pastry Chefs:
Michaël Azouz
Maître Chocolatier, Champion de la Coupe du Monde, Président National du Cercle du Goût Français, Relais Desserts International
Michel Comby
Maître Cuisinier de France, Membre titulaire de l'Académie Culinaire de France, Officier du Mérite agricole, Vainqueur du 1er Trophée Taittinger
Honoré Confiac
Diplome d'Argent e Médaille d'Argent de la Société de Pâtissiers Français, Responsable du Département Boulangerie-Pâtisserie, "Pâtisserie-conseil"/Guadeloups
Olivier Garrivet: Assistant-Pâtissier
Laurent Grégoire: "Meilleur Cookie" (Gault-Millau)
Joël Kichenin
Professeur technique des métiers de bouche, Membre du Groupement Professionnel des Métiers de l'Hôtellerie et de la Restauration/Guadeloupe, Finaliste de la Coupe de France de Pâtisserie 1997, Vainqueur du Trophée du Mérite International 1997
Gérard Lapierre: Chef-Pâtissier
Alain Nonnet
Maître Cuisinier de France, Membre titulaire de l'Académie Culinaire de France, Chevalier de l'Ordre National du Mérite, Officier du Mérite agricole
Nicole et Jean-Baptiste Prades: Chevaliers des Confitureries de France
Frank Saksik: Chef-Pâtissier

Copyright © 1999 for the English edition
Könemann Verlagsgesellschaft mbH
Bonner Straße 126, D-50968 Cologne

Translation from French: Denise Barstow-Girel
English-language editor: Lauren Spirak Johnson
Coordination and typesetting: Agents - Producers - Editors, Overath
Reproduction: Reproservice Werner Pees, Essen
Production manager: Detlev Schaper
Printing and binding: Leefung Asco Printers Ltd., Hong Kong

Printed in China

ISBN 3-8290-2764-8

10 9 8 7 6 5 4 3 2 1

Contents

Foreword

The arts of cooking, baking, and confection-making have always played an integral role in festive occasions the world over, and are an especially important part of French cultural heritage. In recent years the interest in less familiar regions and their culinary traditions has grown. The series *Délices Créole: Exotic Desserts from the French Caribbean* is dedicated to the sweet delicacies of that distant island paradise. The three volumes—Desserts, Cakes, and Confections—reveal a wide array of new and exotic recipes.

Renowned chefs, pastry chefs and confectioners from France and the French territories in the Antilles invite you to discover the delicious possibilities offered by the wide variety of island produce available today. They would like you to explore their culinary world, in which luscious fresh fruits and fragrant spices form the basis of recipes as surprising aas they are succulent. Readily available tropical fruits such as kiwi, pineapples, oranges and melons, as well as lesser-known types such as mangos, carambolas (or star fruits), kumquats and guavas, are used in most of the recipes. These experts have created subtle, daring and sometimes unexpected combinations which are sure to inspire your imagination and teach you something new about the possibilities of marrying taste, color, flavor and fragrance.

Even local products take on a surprisingly exotic flavor when combined with ingredients like curry and cardamom, ginger and aniseed, coconut and rum. From simple sweets to refined delicacies that will delight even the most finicky gourmet, these recipes conjure up images of warm sunshine, sandy beaches, and palm trees.

This collection of recipes takes you on a culinary journey to an exotic island paradise full of vibrant colors, aromas, and fragrances. The detailed step-by-step instructions and color photographs make it easy for you to try the recipes on your own. Suggestions for substitutions and variations in flavors are provided along with the recipes, so your efforts are sure to be successful. In addition, each recipe is accompanied by an informative text describing the culture and tradition of the region or the historical background of a recipe and the origin of its ingredients.

The chefs hope that they have been able to convey their love of their craft in the volumes of this series. Allow yourself to be carried away to the sensuous pleasures of the islands, and spoil your family and guests with some of the finest delicacies paradise has to offer.

Bon appétit!

Jams
and
Preserves

Pineapple, Combava

10 cups/1.5 kg pineapple chunks (about
    2 whole fresh pineapples)
4½ cups/1.125 kg white or brown sugar
1 combava, juiced
1 tsp dried, grated combava rind
2 whole cloves
1 shotglass white rum

Makes	6 jars
Preparation time:	25 minutes
Resting time:	1 hour
Cooking time:	30 minutes
Difficulty:	★

The combava is a type of Caribbean lime with a thick, bumpy green rind. Because of its strong flavor, it should be used sparingly. Too much can overwhelm the more delicate flavor of the pineapple. If combavas are unavailable, ordinary limes may be substituted.

Whole cloves are the buds of the clove tree, picked before blossoming and then dried in the sun. Ideally, they should be freshly ground to a powder before being used in the jam. If this is not possible, substitute ⅛ tsp ready-ground cloves.

The pineapples should be ripe but not overripe, juicy and sweet. Remove and discard any bruised or decayed flesh.

Professional cooks always taste their dishes before adjusting the seasoning. This jam, too, should be tasted to make sure the spices are just right. For a stronger flavor, a bit more dried, grated combava rind may be added, but the amount of cloves should not be increased.

When making jam, the right utensils are extremely important. A large heavy-bottomed copper (not tin-coated) or stainless steel pan should be used, as well as a copper or stainless steel skimmer and a long-handled wooden spoon or heat-proof spatula. The pan must be at least twice the volume of the uncooked jam to prevent boiling over.

It is a good idea to use small jam jars to ensure that, once opened, the jam will be eaten before it has time to spoil. Jars should be thoroughly sterilized according to the manufacturer's instructions.

1. Peel the fresh pineapple, making sure to remove the "eyes," and slice into chunks.

2. Place the pineapple chunks, sugar, and fruit juice in the pan. Let sit for 60 minutes until the sugar has soaked up the juice. Then bring to a boil on high heat, stirring occasionally and skimming regularly. Simmer on moderate heat for 30 minutes.

and Rum Jam

3. Halfway through cooking, add the grated combava rind and the ground cloves.

4. The last time the jam boils, briskly stir in the rum and remove from the heat. Partially blend the jam, leaving a few chunks of fruit. Pour into warm sterilized jars, seal them, and turn upside down until completely cooled. Then turn them right side up again.

Baby Banana

6½ cups/1 kg prepared baby bananas
  (4 lb 4 oz/2 kg whole baby bananas)
3 cups/750 g brown sugar
the juice of 2 limes
scant 1½ cups/125 g dried, grated coconut
1 tbsp nigella seeds
¾ cup/200 ml spring water
a pinch of grated nutmeg

Makes	*4–5 small jars*
Preparation time:	*10 minutes*
Resting time:	*1 hour*
Cooking time:	*20 minutes*
Difficulty:	★

Nowadays any fruit can be found at any time of the year, but jam tastes best when made from the freshest fruit in season. Bananas are harvested year round; however, they are often picked green and sent to ripen in the market, so for this recipe choose only the ripest, sweetest bananas available. Baby bananas may be sold as manzano bananas, which have a refreshing apple-banana flavor. Other sweet bananas such as burro bananas or the familiar yellow Cavendish may be used, but avoid plantains or starchy varieties.

While other kinds of desserts are made for a specific purpose, jam is often made because extra fruit needs to be used up. Fruit for jam should always be of the best quality: just ripe or slightly underripe, firm, free of bruises, blemishes and decay,

and perfectly dry. Wet fruit may harbor mold spores which can cause jam to spoil.

Nigella may be found in Indian markets under the name kalonji, or in Middle Eastern or European markets as charnusshka seeds. Like tomatoes, panatoes, and tobacco, it is a member of the nightshade family, and its small black seeds are known for their distinctive aromatic flavor. Combined with the nutmeg, they add an exotic fragrance to the bananas.

Purists use bottled spring water for making jams and jellies. If this is not practical, here is a tip to get rid of the chemical taste of tap water: Leave the required amount of tap water (plus a bit extra to allow for evaporation) in a shallow uncovered dish overnight. The chlorine will naturally evaporate.

1. Peel the bananas, slice into chunks, and put them in the preserving pan. Add the sugar, lime juice and water, and stir. Let sit 60 minutes until the sugar has soaked up all the juices, stirring occasionally.

2. If using whole nutmeg, finely grate it with a grater, spice mill or hand-held coffee grinder.

and Coconut Jam

3. Add the coconut to the banana mixture, and bring to a boil over low heat, stirring constantly. Skim as necessary. Cook for 20 minutes on moderate heat.

4. Add the nigella seeds and nutmeg 10 minutes before the end of cooking, and continue stirring. While the jam is still boiling, fill the warm sterilized jars and seal them. Turn upside down to cool, but turn them right side up again before they have cooled completely.

Cucumber, Passion Fruit

6½ cups/1 kg prepared cucumbers
   (about 2 lb 12 oz/1.25 kg whole
   cucumbers)
4⅔ cups/700 g passion fruit
3 cups/750 g brown sugar
1 tsp caraway seed
2 tbsp agar-agar powder

Makes   *6 small jars*
Preparation time: *30 minutes*
Resting time: *15 minutes*
Cooking time: *30 minutes*
Difficulty: ★

This combination of ordinary mild cucumbers and sweetly sour passion fruit, spiced up with the surprise of caraway, is both zesty and tropical.

Caraway is the "secret" ingredient in this recipe. Its slightly bitter taste is often used in counterpoint to the sweetness of pastries and breads. It can also be found in liqueurs and has traditional medicinal uses. This jam contrasts the pungent caraway and the naturally low-calorie cucumbers with exuberant passion fruit, which should be as ripe and juicy as possible.

Best for this recipe are the long "English" or hothouse cucumbers, with few seeds and a firm meaty texture. Other types of cucumbers can be used, such as the kiwano or prickly cucumber, an exotic yellowish variety which is usually egg-shaped and covered with hard pointy prickles like a horse chestnut. The flavor is a bit sour and salty, and the seeds are smaller but more numerous, adding an attractive visual touch and even a delicate almond taste to the jam.

Agar-agar is a natural gelling agent derived from dried seaweed. It is very effective in helping liquids set, without affecting their texture or flavor. It comes in powder or flake form and may be sold in candy-supply shops. If it is hard to find, pectin or powdered gelatin may be substituted, but tend to be less effective or pleasing in texture than the agar-agar.

After the jam has been poured into the jars, for added flavor and decoration, sprinkle a few caraway seeds onto the surface before sealing them.

1. Wash, peel and thinly slice the cucumbers. Cut the passion fruits in half. Scoop out the pulp, including seeds, and strain it through a sieve, food mill or juicer to extract the juice.

2. Pour half the passion fruit juice into a large bowl with the cucumbers, add the sugar, stir briskly and let sit 15 minutes until the sugar has soaked up the juices.

and Caraway Jam

3. Bring to a boil over moderate heat and continue cooking for 20 minutes. Stir regularly and skim occasionally. Purée about half of the mixture using a beater, blender or food processor.

4. Add the remaining passion fruit juice and the caraway and simmer for another 10 minutes. Several minutes before cooking time is up, add the agar-agar and whisk until dissolved. Pour the boiling jam into warm sterilized jars, seal and turn upside down. Turn them right side up before they have cooled completely.

Cherimoya, Guava

4 cups/600 g cherimoya pulp
  (about 2 lb 14 oz/1.3 kg whole fruit)
2⅔ cups/400 g guavas
3 cups/750 g brown sugar
the juice of 1 lime
2 tsp ground coriander

Makes	*6 small jars*
Preparation time:	*20 minutes*
Resting time:	*1 hour*
Cooking time:	*25 minutes*
Difficulty:	*★*

The cherimoya, also known as custard-apple, is a tropical fruit which grows particularly well in the Antilles. It is delicious, rich in vitamin C and minerals, and is becoming widely available in the United States now that it is being grown in California. It is roughly egg-shaped, with a scaly pale green rind and creamy white pulp containing very hard black seeds. When ripe, the rind yields gently to finger pressure, and the velvety flesh tastes like pineapple, bananas and strawberries combined.

Coriander, originally from Asia, is an herb with sweet spicy seeds in a thin shell. The seeds are green when unripe and turn white or beige when ripe. They are used for different culinary purposes depending on the stage; green seeds are used in gingerbread or in distilling gin. For this recipe, grind whole ripe seeds or use the ready-ground coriander available in most supermarkets. It should have a bright sharp fragrance; if it is dusty it will mar the finished jam.

All spices taste best when freshly ground, and a spice mill or small coffee grinder is ideal for this purpose. Blenders and food processors work well only for grinding large quantitites. For best flavor, add the spices to the jam just a few minutes before the end of cooking.

It is important to stir constantly so the jam does not stick to the bottom of the kettle, especially when the fruit is puréed, as it tends to stick more easily.

1. Wash the cherimoyas. Cut them in half and scoop out the pulp, then remove the seeds.

2. Wash the guavas, peel them, and strain the pulp through a sieve or food mill. Put the cherimoya and guava pulp in a large preserving pan, add the sugar and the lime juice, and stir. Let sit for 60 minutes until the sugar has soaked up the juice.

and Coriander Jam

3. Bring to a boil and cook over moderate heat for 20 minutes, stirring constantly and skimming as needed.

4. Add the coriander and cook another 5 minutes. Pour the jam into sterilized jars, seal and turn upside down. Turn them right side up before they have cooled completely.

Kiwano and

6½ cups/1 kg kiwano pulp
3 cups/750 g brown sugar
the juice of 1 lime
2 tsp ground star anise

Makes   *4 small jars*
Preparation time: *20 minutes*
Resting time: *1 hour*
Cooking time: *25 minutes*
Difficulty: ★

Kiwanos, also called horned melons or prickly cucumbers, are increasingly available in North America. They are usually sold alongside other melons in fine grocers and supermarkets. Orange, oblong and spiny, they look exotic and decorative. The pale green flesh tastes like our familiar cucumbers, but with a limey tang, and they are full of potassium. Only the ripest melons, with a bright orange color, should be used. The larger and fleshier they are, the tastier.

In this recipe, white sugar could be substituted for brown, but is less flavorful. Brown cane sugar has a slight vanilla aroma that enhances the flavor of the fruit. It is also important to be very careful when cooking with sugar. Sugar not only becomes much hotter than boiling water, but also sticks to the skin. To prevent burns, always use long-handled utensils and wear potholders or oven mitts.

In this jam, the dominant flavor is the star anise. Its licorice aroma is a perfect complement to the kiwanos, enhancing their taste, and also aiding digestion. This combination is an original and very pleasant surprise to the palate.

It is important to include the kiwano seeds in the jam, not only for visual appeal and taste, but also because they develop a delicious almond flavor after a few weeks.

1. Peel the kiwanos and cut into slices ¼–½ in/5 mm thick, making sure to reserve the seeds. Put the slices in large preserving pan.

2. Add the brown sugar and lime juice. Let sit for 20 minutes, until the sugar has soaked up the juices. Stir occasionally.

Star Anise Jam

3. Bring to a boil, then cook for 20 minutes on moderate heat. Add the ground star anise a few minutes before the end of cooking, and stir briskly.

4. Pour out one ladle of the boiling jam into a pretty serving dish. Pour the rest of the jam into warm sterilized jars, seal and turn upside down. Let cool before turning right side up.

Mauritius

6½ cups/1 kg peeled, cored Asian pears
    (about 3 lb 5 oz/1.5 kg whole fruit)
3¾ cups/900 g brown sugar
the juice of 1 lime
1⅓ cups/200 g prepared fresh lychees
1 tsp ground cinnamon
1 cinnamon stick, broken into 7 or 8 pieces
1 tsp ground black pepper
a glass of water

Makes	4 small jars
Preparation time:	20 minutes
Resting time:	1 hour
Cooking time:	45 minutes
Difficulty:	★

Imagine the delight when your family and friends taste this extraordinary jam.

It is important to use a heavy non-reactive pan when making jam. This avoids chemical reactions with the food, and the heavy bottom heats evenly to prevent sticking. Enameled pans may be scorched by hot sugar, while the acid in the fruit can corrode ironware.

The quantity of fruit in jam recipes is usually for washed, peeled and cored or pitted fruit, so precise measurement is crucial. For this recipe fresh, ripe lychees should be purchased; about 30 whole ones will do. Their natural sweetness complements the delicate, mild flavor of the Asian pears. If fresh lychees are unavailable, substitute drained canned lychees, which do not need to be cooked in sugar syrup. Do not use lychee nuts, which are dry and hard.

A trick of the trade is to cook the seeds and cores along with the fruit, enclosed in a cheesecloth bag. The bag is tied to the handle of the preserving pan so that it can easily be removed later. If the pan has no handle, simply place the bag in the jam, but be sure to use a heatproof utensil when removing it. The seeds are crucial because during cooking they release a substance called pectin, which helps the jam to gel. When the fruit has finished cooking, the cheesecloth bag is wrung out over the pot to release all the essential juices into the jam. The fruit is then partially puréed to provide an interesting mix of textures before adding the whole lychees.

1. Peel, core and thinly slice the Asian pears. Set aside the cores and seeds. Put the slices in the preserving pan and sprinkle with the lime juice. Add 3½ cups/850 g of the sugar. Let sit for 1 hour so the sugar can soak up the fruit juices.

2. Put the reserved cores and seeds in a cheesecloth, close with a string, and tie the string to the pot handle so the bag sits in the fruit mixture. Bring the jam to a boil over moderate heat, then cook on high heat for 15 minutes. Remove the cheesecloth bag, and squeeze over the pan. Then purée part of the jam in the blender or food processor, and return it to the pot.

Jam

3. Peel and pit the lychees. Make a sugar syrup by boiling a glass of water and the remaining sugar. Cook the lychees in the syrup for 5–8 minutes.

4. When the jam is cooked, add the lychees, ground cinnamon, cinnamon pieces and freshly ground pepper. Bring to a boil again, and cook the jam another 15 minutes, stirring regularly. While still boiling, pour into sterilized jars, seal and turn upside down. Turn right side up before they have cooled completely.

Mango

6½ cups/1 kg peeled, pitted mangoes
   (about 4 whole mangoes)
3⅓ cups/500 g peeled, seeded, chopped
   pumpkin
5⅔ cups/1.125 g brown sugar
the juice of 1 lime
10 drops almond extract
1 cinnamon stick, broken into 5 or 6 pieces
a pinch of agar-agar powder

Makes	*6 small jars*
Preparation time:	*40 minutes*
Resting time:	*1 hour*
Cooking time:	*30 minutes*
Difficulty:	★

Gourmets and others will enjoy this exotic jam at any time of day: for breakfast on toast, with afternoon tea or coffee on scones, even as a dessert sauce on cake, ice cream or fruit salad. Let your imagination run wild! One thing is for sure: Jam tastes better when homemade. It is well worth the effort to make jam when tropical fruit are at their best, so the taste of tropical sunshine can be appreciated on a cold, rainy day.

Just the sight of the jewel-like shades of orange and yellow will brighten your day. Mangoes and pumpkins are of course very different in flavor, but the same guidelines should be used for choosing them: the best quality, ripe but still firm. If they are too soft, they will turn to mush during cooking and will not be as pleasantly textured. The jam will be much more enjoyable if the chunks retain their shape and are ever so slightly crunchy. This means paying close attention so as not to overcook the fruit, and also making sure the jam does not stick to the bottom of the pot. The jam should be stirred and skimmed regularly to remove the particles that rise to the surface.

The lime juice both helps the jam to gel and adds a tang that brings out the best in the other fruits.

One more special touch is to add a few blanched almonds to the top of each pot of jam before sealing. These look very elegant and add an extra crunch to this suave combination. Serve the jam on yellow cake for an attractive and delicious treat.

1. Peel, seed and chop the pumpkin into small chunks. Put them into a large preserving pan, then add the sugar and lime juice. Stir and set aside for 1 hour.

2. Peel the mangoes, then vertically slice half the fruit about ½ in/1 cm from the midpoint. Turn the mango and repeat on the other side, avoiding the large fibrous stone in the center. Slice the halves thinly, add to the pumpkin and stir briskly. Bring to a boil over low heat, stirring gently. Cook 15 minutes more on high heat. Stir often and skim occasionally.

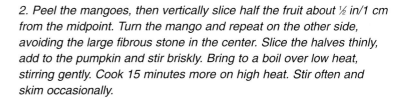

Pumpkin Jam

3. Add the cinnamon pieces, and simmer on moderate heat for another 15 minutes.

4. The last time the mixture boils, add the almond extract and agar-agar and stir briskly. Remove from the heat, and while it is still boiling, pour the jam into sterilized jars, seal and turn upside down. Let cool before turning them right side up.

Mango, Red Wine

10⅔ cups/1.6 kg prepared mangoes
   (about 6 whole mangoes)
the juice of 1 lime
4½ cups/1.2 kg brown sugar
1 cup/250 ml red wine
½ tsp ground cinnamon
3 tsp ground coriander

Makes	6–8 small jars
Preparation time:	15 minutes
Resting time:	1 hour 30 minutes
Cooking time:	30 minutes
Difficulty:	★ ★

It may be surprising to learn that wine is a very common ingredient in all kinds of recipes. The type of wine selected, however, must marry well with the dish. A full-bodied red wine is a perfect foil for this jam because it complements the sweetness of the mangoes. Do not use so-called "cooking wine," which will spoil the fresh flavor of the fruit.

The mangoes should be ripe but still firm, because overly soft mangoes will turn mushy during cooking and the jam will not look as good. Firm, tasty, fruity chunks will make the jam look more appetizing.

Coriander is the seed of a pungent herb, the breathy fragrant leaves of which are better known as cilantro. The Romans used it as a medicinal plant, and Charlemagne recommended growing it for culinary and medicinal uses as a tonic, an antiseptic and also an aid to digestion. The seeds are traditionally added to sauces and stews made with wine.

Add the coriander once the jam has begun to thicken, just before the end of cooking, so the spice does not have time to evaporate or lose its distinctive fragrance.

Those who enjoy strong bursts of flavor may wish to add a few whole grains of coriander to the top of each jar before closing and sealing them.

1. Peel, pit and thinly slice the mangoes and then place them in the preserving pan.

2. Add the lime juice, sugar, red wine and cinnamon, stir and set aside for 1½ hours.

and Coriander Jam

3. Gradually bring to a boil, then simmer for 20 minutes on high heat, stirring and skimming regularly. Remove from the heat, purée part of the jam in a blender or food processor, then return it to the pan.

4. Add the coriander and continue to simmer for 10 minutes while stirring energetically. Pour the boiling jam into jars, seal them, and invert them to cool. Turn them right side up only after they have completely cooled.

Cantaloupe

10 cups/1.5 kg prepared cantaloupe
   (about 4 lb 6 oz/2 kg whole melon)
3⅓ cups/500 g peeled kiwis
   (5 or 6 whole kiwis)
6 cups/1.5 kg brown sugar
1½ tsp ground cinnamon
⅔ cup/150 ml Shrubb liqueur
1½ tsp agar-agar powder

Makes	6 small jars
Preparation time:	15 minutes
Resting time:	1 hour
Cooking time:	30 minutes
Difficulty:	★

When making jam, it is important to adapt the amount of sugar to the quantity of fruit, maintaining the proportion of 2 lb 3 oz/ 1 kilogram of fruit for 3 cups/750 grams of sugar. The quantities may of course be varied depending how much fruit you wish to use, but the proportions must always be respected. Too little sugar can cause the jam to ferment, and too much sugar can make it crystallize.

The combination of kiwi and cantaloupe—two sweet, full-flavored fruits pleasant to the bite—is delightful. The kiwi adds a tangy flavor, while the agar-agar helps the jam to gel.

For this recipe, ground cinnamon is preferable to whole cinnamon sticks because it blends much better with the flavor of

this jam. In either form, the cinnamon must be added at the end of cooking, so that its fragrance remains fresh and strong.

Shrubb is the name of a Caribbean liqueur made of orange or tangerine peels steeped in rum, but another orange liqueur such as Cointreau, Grand Marnier or Triple Sec can easily be substituted if it proves difficult to obtain.

Jam will normally keep for a long time if it is hermetically sealed and stored in a cool, dry, dark place. Because jam tends to shrink as it cools, it is important to fill the jars as close to the brim as possible before sealing them.

1. Wash the cantaloupe, cut in half and scoop out the seeds. Peel and dice, then check the weight to be sure it is the right amount.

2. Peel and cut the kiwis into thin slices. Put all the fruit into the preserving pan, add the sugar and stir. Let sit for 1 hour until the sugar has soaked up the fruit juices. Stir regularly.

Kiwi Shrubb Jam

3. Bring to a boil and simmer on moderate heat for 30 minutes, stirring and skimming occasionally.

4. A few minutes before the end of cooking, sprinkle the cinnamon, Shrubb and agar-agar on the jam, then stir briskly. Remove from the heat, and while still boiling, pour the jam into sterilized jars, seal, and turn upside down. Turn right side up while still warm.

Watermelon Cantaloupe

5 cups/750 g prepared watermelon
   (about 3 lb 5 oz/1.5 kg whole melon)
5 cups/750 g prepared cantaloupe
   (about 3 lb 5 oz/1.5 kg whole melon)
4½ cups/1.125 kg brown or white sugar
the juice of 1 lime
2 tsp freshly ground black pepper
1 bunch fresh peppermint
1 tsp agar-agar powder

Makes	*6 small jars*
Preparation time:	*30 minutes*
Resting time:	*30 minutes*
Cooking time:	*30 minutes*
Difficulty:	*★*

Successful homemade jam has a long shelf-life. Using the right amount of sugar is the key to making jam that keeps well, without either crystallizing or fermenting. The amount of sugar may be adjusted depending on the type of fruit. If a very juicy fruit is used, the sugar can be increased slightly, but if the fruit naturally contains a lot of pectin, the sugar will need to be reduced slightly. The sugar, acid and pectin in the fruit, added to the other ingredients in the recipe, are balanced to ensure that the jam sets properly.

Another key to success is the quality of the fruit. It should be just ripe enough but not too ripe; always avoid purchasing large quantities of overripe fruit for jam-making. The best jam comes from fruits that are just right, full of flavor but not past their prime.

The quantity of fruit is also important. Buy a generous amount of whole fruit and carefully measure after it is peeled, seeded and chopped. To avoid running short, put double the amount of prepared fruit on your shopping list, for example, two pounds whole melon for each pound prepared.

The watermelon in this jam is included especially to heighten the color. Equal quantities of watermelon and cantaloupe provide bright color and a perfect balance of melon flavor.

1. Cut the watermelon and the cantaloupe in crescents. Remove the rinds and seeds, and dice.

2. Put the fruit in the preserving pan, add the sugar and lime juice and let sit for 30 minutes, stirring occasionally.

Peppermint-Pepper Jam

3. Bring to a boil on high heat, then simmer for 20 minutes, stirring and skimming regularly. Purée part of the jam in a blender or food processor, then mix it back into the pan.

4. Add the pepper and the washed and dried peppermint, tied in a bunch. Stir and simmer on moderate heat for another 10 minutes. 5 minutes before the end of cooking, remove the peppermint and sprinkle the agar-agar on the jam, stirring briskly. While still boiling, pour into sterilized jars, seal and turn upside down. Turn right side up while still warm.

Sweet Potato

6½ cups/1 kg peeled sweet potatoes
3 cups/750 g brown sugar
the juice of 2 limes
6⅓ cups/1.5 liters spring water
3 tbsp ground turmeric
2 shotglasses aged rum

Makes	4–5 small jars
Preparation time:	20 minutes
Resting time:	1 hour 30 minutes
Cooking time:	35 minutes
Difficulty:	★

Sweet potatoes are a kind of tropical tuber in the volubilis family. They are often sold as yams, though technically they are not the same thing. The skin color can vary from yellow to white to red and even purplish, and the flesh is white, not yellow. They are often cooked as a vegetable, but are also used in sweet dishes, candies and jams. If they are unavailable, then the better known orange-fleshed sweet potatoes may be substituted.

Turmeric is also known as "poor man's saffron," and it comes from a rhizome in the ginger family. It is often used in curries for its bright yellow color and its distinctive flavor. For this recipe, use dried ground turmeric rather than the fresh whole root.

Letting the fruit sit for a while is an important stage in making jam, because it allows the sugar to absorb the juices and thus the flavors of the fruit. In this recipe, the acidic lime juice not only prevents the sweet potatoes from oxidizing and turning black, but also adds a crisp, tangy flavor.

It is very important to turn the jam jars upside down immediately once they have been closed because the boiling jam heats the lids. This makes the metal expand, ensuring a tight, sterile seal and thus a long shelf-life.

Enjoy this jam as a relish with curries, or as an alternative, with jerked or roast meats.

1. Wash, peel, and grate the sweet potatoes.

2. Put the grated sweet potatoes in a large preserving pan. Add the sugar, lime juice, and water, and soak for 1½ hours. Stir occasionally.

Turmeric Jam

3. Cook on moderate heat for 20 minutes, stirring and skimming regularly. Add the turmeric and stir. Cook for another 15 minutes.

4. The last time the jam boils, add the rum and stir. While still boiling, pour into warm sterilized jars, seal and turn upside down to cool. Turn right side up while still lukewarm.

Tamarillo, Onion

4⅔ cups/700 g tamarillos or
　ordinary tomatoes
2 cups/300 g prepared onions
3 cups/750 g brown sugar
2 combavas
½ tsp grated nutmeg

Makes	*5 small jars*
Preparation time:	*20 minutes*
Resting time::	*15 minutes*
Cooking time:	*30 minutes*
Difficulty:	★

Tamarillos, also known as tree tomatoes, are actually a sweet and sour fruit that is not a tomato at all! They are tart and refreshing and grow in a stunning array of colors ranging from golden yellow to dark red. Tamarillos should be used when very ripe, and the skin should be peeled, as it tends to be tough and bitter. The seeds may also be discarded; this is a question of preference. Tamarillos may be found in fine grocers or Latino markets, but if they are unavailable, use ordinary tomatoes.

Combavas are a citrus fruit like limes, but smaller and rounder, with a thick, bumpy rind and a much stronger flavor.

If they are hard to find, common limes may be substituted. In this recipe, not all of the grated rind will be needed, so what is left over may be dried and ground and saved for later use. It will keep perfectly in a tightly closed jar. Combava rind has a very strong taste; use it with caution so as not to overwhelm the other flavors in the jam.

Onions are used in this recipe because they add bite and a slight acidity to balance the tamarillo flavor. They also add a bit more texture to the jam.

1. Peel the tamarillos or tomatoes, and slice thinly. Do not remove the seeds.

2. Peel the onions and slice lengthwise in matchsticks.

and Combava Jam

3. Grate the citrus rind, then squeeze the juice. Put the tamarillos and onions in the preserving pan, add the juice and sugar, and stir briskly. Set aside for 15 minutes, stirring regularly.

4. Bring to a boil, then add the nutmeg and a pinch of the grated rind. Let simmer on moderate heat for 30 minutes, stirring regularly. While still boiling, pour into sterilized jars, seal and turn upside down to cool. Turn right side up while still lukewarm.

Tomato

6 cups/1.5 kg tomato juice
  (11 lb/5 kg whole tomatoes)
4½ cups/1.125 kg brown sugar
juice of 1 lime or 1 lemon
1½ tbsp/20 g whole cardamom pods
6½ tbsp/100 ml lychee liqueur
1½ tsp agar-agar powder

Makes	*5 small jars*
Preparation time:	*30 minutes*
Cooking time:	*45 minutes*
Difficulty:	★

This jam creates a unique harmony between the acidity of tomatoes and the aromatic sweetness of lychee liqueur, set off nicely by the unusual, almost peppery flavor of cardamom.

The jam will taste best if the tomatoes are perfectly ripe. Cherry tomatoes or vine-ripened hothouse tomatoes work well, and fresh farmstand or home-grown tomatoes are superb. Avoid out-of-season supermarket tomatoes, which are picked green and then gassed to simulate ripeness. Using ready-made tomato juice is temptingly easy, but the flavor will not be the same, and it often contains preservatives that are best avoided.

Fresh cardamom pods are easy to shell and grind, though pre-shelled cardamom seeds are most convenient if available. Ready ground cardamom may be used as long as it is fresh and fragrant. Have the cardamom shelled and ready to use before you begin to cook the jam. For an extra burst of flavor, set aside a few whole seeds to add to each jar before sealing.

The cooking times for this recipe should be strictly observed so that the sugar does not burn, which would cause the tomatoes to darken unappealingly.

1. Wash the whole tomatoes, dry them, dice and put through a juicer, food processor, blender or sieve.

2. Put the tomato juice in the preserving pan. Add the sugar and citrus juice. Bring to a boil, stir occasionally, and skim any particles that rise to the surface. Simmer for 15 minutes.

Lychee Liqueur Jam

3. Shell the cardamom pods. Discard the papery hulls, set aside a few grains, and grind the rest with a mortar and pestle or peppermill. Add the ground cardamom to the jam and cook for another 15 minutes.

4. Add the lychee liqueur and the agar-agar and stir briskly. Cook 5 more minutes, then remove from heat. While still boiling, pour the jam into warm sterilized jars, seal and turn upside down. Turn right side up while still lukewarm.

Creole Delight

6½ cups/1 kg peeled oranges (about
  4 lb 6 oz/2 kg whole oranges)
3 cups/750 g brown sugar
the juice of 1 lime
6 whole cloves
2 vanilla beans
¾ tsp agar-agar powder

Makes	6 small jars
Preparation time:	*30 minutes*
Resting time:	*1 hour*
Cooking time:	*40 minutes*
Difficulty:	★

This aromatic marmalade is as distinct from the usual super-market varieties as fine champagne is from club soda.

Oranges are naturally sweet and juicy but have a very thick bitter rind and white pith, which should be carefully and thoroughly removed so the jam does not become bitter.

Vanilla beans are in fact the fruit of a kind of orchid, but they undergo several processing steps before acquiring their characteristic black-brown color and heavenly fragrance. In this recipe, vanilla balances the strong spicy taste of cloves.

Cloves have been known since before the Roman era, and during the Middle Ages were used for medicinal as well as culinary purposes. Cloves were stuck in oranges not just to make scented pomanders (a sort of medieval air freshener), but also because they were believed to protect people from the dreaded plague. Use cloves sparingly in cooking; oil of cloves is a topical anesthetic!

Puréeing part of the jam halfway through cooking, then mixing it with the rest, gives the jam a lovely smooth texture, while leaving some luscious chunks of fruit to please the eye and the palate. A hand-held electric blender does the job in a minute, without even having to go to the trouble of removing the fruit from the pan. Enjoy!

1. Peel the oranges and remove the white pith. Slice thinly and put in the preserving pan.

2. Add the sugar, lime juice, and cloves. Cut the vanilla beans into small pieces and add those. Let sit for 1 hour.

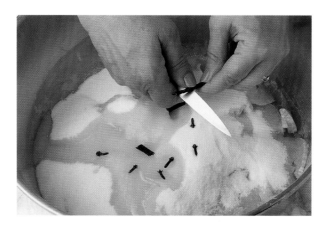

Orange Marmalade

3. Bring to a boil on moderate heat, then simmer 40 minutes. Stir occasionally and skim regularly. Halfway through cooking, purée part of the jam. 5 minutes before the end, sprinkle the agar-agar onto the jam and stir well.

4. While still boiling, pour into sterilized jars, making sure each jar gets its share of cloves and vanilla pieces. Seal the jars and turn upside down to cool. Turn right side up while still lukewarm.

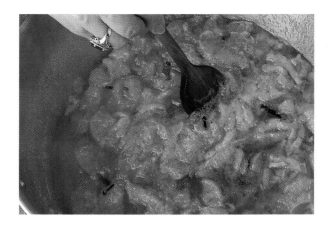

Papaya

4 cups/1 liter papaya juice
  (4 lb 6 oz/2 kg whole papayas)
3 cups/750 g brown sugar
2 shotglasses aged rum
the juice of 2 large oranges
3 tsp grains of paradise
½ tsp agar-agar flakes

Makes	*6 small jars*
Preparation time:	*25 minutes*
Resting time:	*15 minutes*
Cooking time:	*40 minutes*
Difficulty:	★

This enchanting jam tastes of distilled sunlight. It is easy to make, when fresh papayas and oranges are available, and the flavor is both refined and lingering.

Grains of paradise, or maniguette, are the seeds of an African plant that produces beautiful flowers. The seeds are very spicy and hot because they contain the same essential oil as pepper. They have been used medicinally since time immemorial and in the Middle Ages were a sought after substitute for the rarer black pepper. These days, grains of paradise may be more difficult to find; freshly ground black pepper can be substituted.

Papaya Paradise Preserves tastes best made with freshly squeezed orange juice, so for this recipe only the sweetest, ripest, juiciest oranges will do. The papayas should be as ripe as possible, but still firm. Peeled, cut fruit changes color when it reacts to oxygen. To avoid discoloration, cover the fruit completely with juice and sugar before setting aside.

Fine rum enhances the fruit flavors and adds a hint of the exotic island lifestyle. Savor every drop of this taste of paradise!

1. Peel and seed the papayas, dice, and put the chunks in the preserving pan.

2. Add the sugar, rum, and orange juice. Stir briskly. Let the mixture sit for 15 minutes, stirring occasionally.

Paradise Preserves

3. Bring to a boil, then simmer 30 minutes on moderate heat. Stir now and then and skim regularly. After 20 minutes, add the spice and stir briskly. Purée part of the jam with a blender or food processor.

4. For the last 10 minutes of cooking, stir constantly. Add the agar-agar just before the end and mix well. While still boiling, pour into sterilized jars. Seal and turn upside down. Turn right side up when completely cooled.

13 cups/2 kg pepino pulp
   (about 5 lb 13 oz/2.7 kg whole pepinos)
6 cups/1.5 kg sugar
the juice of 2 limes
3 tsp fresh grated gingerroot
½ tsp ground cinnamon
1¾ tsp agar-agar powder

Makes	*6 small jars*
Preparation time:	*25 minutes*
Resting time:	*1 hour*
Cooking time:	*35 minutes*
Difficulty:	*★*

Pepinos, or melon pears, are what makes this jam extra special. This South American fruit is a type of bush melon with a tangy taste reminiscent of honeydew and cucumber. Pepinos are oval, about 2½ to 3½ inches (6 to 8 centimeters) long. They are a soft yellow color with brownish streaks, and turn a speckled eggplant color when ripe. Look for them next to the melons or in the exotic produce section of fine grocers and supermarkets.

Ginger is an aromatic tuber with a refreshing bite to the taste, widely used in Asian dishes and wonderful for heightening the flavors of fruit. Fresh gingerroot is readily found at supermarkets and ethnic grocers. Do not substitute the ground dried root; it does not have the same crisp taste and fragrance. The amount should not be increased, either, or it will overpower the delicate blend of fruit and cinnamon.

The key to success with this jam is to allow the full resting time for the sugar to fully absorb all the flavor from the fruit and juices. The fruit mix can even be left longer than an hour; it will only taste better. When it is cooking, the jam should be watched carefully and stirred often, to make sure it does not stick.

1. Wash and peel the pepinos, slice thinly, and put in the preserving pan. Add the sugar and lime juice. Stir the mixture and let it sit for 1 hour until the sugar has absorbed all the juices.

2. Peel, grate, and reserve the fresh ginger root. Bring the fruit mixture to a boil. Stir regularly and skim occasionally. Simmer for 20 minutes on moderate heat. Purée part of the jam with a blender or food processor.

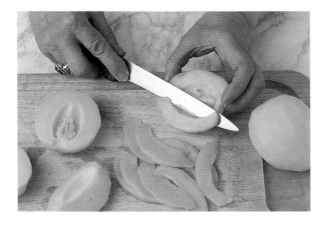

Ginger Jam

3. Add the ginger and cinnamon. Cook another 15 minutes, stirring often. Sprinkle the agar-agar onto the jam just before the end of cooking and stir until it is well blended.

4. While the jam is still boiling, fill the sterilized jars, seal and turn upside down. Turn right side up while still lukewarm.

6½ cups/1 kg peeled tangerines (generous
　　3 lb 5 oz/1.5 kg whole tangerines)
3 cups/750 g white or brown sugar
2 tsp jasmine green tea leaves
1 tbsp agar-agar powder

Makes	*6 small jars*
Preparation time:	*20 minutes*
Resting time:	*30 minutes*
Cooking time:	*30 minutes*
Difficulty:	★

Tangerines are at their peak around Christmas time, and this recipe celebrates the delights of filling the home with the wonderful aromas of holiday cooking.

This jam is an unusual and delicious blend of jasmine tea and tangerines. The tangerine is a kind of mandarin orange first grown by an Algerian monk at the beginning of the 20th century. Father Clément created a hybrid of an orange and a mandarin fruit, so in French it was named after him, *clémentine*. In English, the name "tangerine" may come from the Algerian city of Tangiers. By whatever name, they are sweet and sour, bursting with flavor, and should be chosen ripe but still firm.

Jasmine tea is famed for its perfumed taste. For this jam, green leaf jasmine tea should be used, because it is more delicately flavored than black tea. Many exotic types of tea are now available (for example, passion fruit tea, coconut tea, apricot tea, ginger tea, vanilla tea and so on). There is no harm in experimenting with other teas in this recipe, but jasmine tea adds a beautiful fragrance and a definitive oriental gloss to this delicious tropical jam.

Naturally, this jam should be served with hot jasmine tea.

1. Peel the tangerines, separate into segments, and put in the preserving pan. Add the sugar and stir. Let sit 30 minutes.

2. Bring to a boil over high heat, then simmer for 20 minutes on moderate heat. Stir and skim occasionally. Halfway through cooking, purée part of the jam with a blender or food processor.

Orient Jam

3. Add the tea leaves, blend well, then simmer 10 more minutes.

4. A few minutes before the end of cooking, sprinkle the agar-agar onto the jam and stir thoroughly. While the jam is still boiling, fill the sterilized jars, seal and turn upside down. Turn the jars right side up while still lukewarm.

4⅓ cups/650 g starfruit
scant 9 cups/1.35 kg prepared giraumon
the juice of 1 lime
6 cups/1.5 kg brown sugar
6 tbsp/90 g grated fresh gingerroot

Makes	*8 small jars*
Preparation time:	*30 minutes*
Resting time:	*1 hour*
Cooking time:	*35 minutes*
Difficulty:	★

Giraumon is a type of hard orange-fleshed squash grown in the Antilles. It should be very ripe for the best flavor and texture. If it is not ripe enough, it will be stringy and hard to dice. Look for it in West Indian or Latino markets, but if it is not available, try substituting Japanese pumpkin (smaller than the American variety, with a greenish rind) or butternut squash.

Starfruit have different names on different Caribbean islands. For example, they are also known as carambola, bilimbi, and five-finger, and have a sweet/sour, juicy flavor. Typically pale green to yellow, they are the size and shape of small cucumbers, but with five ridges which give slices of the fruit a characteristic star shape.

Stir this jam regularly during cooking to blend the two types of fruit well, and to evenly distribute the spicy ginger. Do not substitute ground ginger for fresh. The lime juice can be replaced with lemon juice, but no other type of citrus should be used, as the flavor would be disappointing. White sugar may substitute for the brown, if necessary, but it is best to avoid experimenting with other types of sugars, for the flavor and color of the jam would be affected.

Make sure the jam jars are completely cool before affixing labels to them; otherwise, the labels will fall off.

1. Peel the squash, seed, and dice. Wash the starfruit, then cut off the black tips. Cut the starfruit in ¼–½ inch/5 mm thick slices, making attractive star shapes. Reserve 10 "stars" for decoration.

2. In the preserving pan, combine the diced squash, carambola, lime juice, and sugar. Stir gently and let sit for 1 hour.

Jam

3. Bring the mixture to a boil and cook on high heat 35 minutes. Stir often and skim occasionally.

4. Halfway through cooking, add the ginger. Remove from the heat, partially purée the jam, then bring back to a boil. Fill the sterilized jars with hot jam, decorating each with a reserved "star," either placed on top, or slid down inside a wall to be visible from the side. Seal the jars and turn upside down. When cool, turn right side up again.

Creole Lady

6½ cups/1 kg peeled grapefruit
5 cups/750 g peeled bananas
generous ¾ cup/125 g peeled kiwis
3½ oz/100 g kumquats
6 cups/1.5 kg brown sugar
2 vanilla beans
1 shotglass aged rum

Makes	6 small jars
Preparation time:	35 minutes
Resting time:	30 minutes
Cooking time:	35 minutes
Difficulty:	★

The fruit recommended in this recipe can be varied, but the balance of sweet and sour should be maintained. In this case, the slight tart bitterness of the grapefruit is counteracted by the soft sweet flavor of the kiwis and bananas, which are in turn enhanced by the assertive tang of kumquats. Any citrus fruit can be substituted for the grapefruit, but remember to remove both the peel and the white pith, to prevent its bitterness from affecting the finished jam.

The bananas should be firm and ripe. Sprinkle the sliced banana with lime or lemon juice to prevent discoloration and add extra flavor.

Jam normally sets at a temperature of 225 °F/108 °C. To test for doneness without a jelly or candy thermometer, try this trick: Put a small ceramic plate in the refrigerator or freezer to chill. When the jam has cooked, spoon a few drops on the plate and leave it for one minute to cool. Then touch the jam with a fingertip. If the jam wrinkles, it is ready to set.

The vanilla beans are usually removed at the end of cooking, but for an exotic decorative touch they can be cut in sections. Add one piece to each jar, positioned vertically on the inside of a wall. With a pretty cover, these jars of jam make a perfect housewarming gift or a very personal holiday present.

1. Peel the grapefruit and carefully remove the white pith. Cut the grapefruit into chunks. Peel and slice the bananas. Peel and dice the kiwis.

2. Wash the kumquats. Halve them and remove the seeds. Place in a pan of cold water, bring to a boil on high heat, and blanch for 5 minutes. Meanwhile, add the grapefruit, bananas, kiwis and sugar to the preserving pan and let sit 30 minutes, stirring regularly.

Marmalade

3. Cut the blanched kumquats in thin rounds and add them to the pan. Bring to a boil over low heat. Stir and skim occasionally. Add the vanilla pieces to the fruit mixture, then cook on high heat 30 minutes longer. Continue to stir and skim now and then.

4. At the end of cooking, briskly stir in the rum and remove the pan from the heat. Fill the sterilized jars immediately, adding the decorative vanilla pieces, if desired. Seal the jars and turn upside down. When lukewarm, turn right side up.

Cape Gooseberry

4 cups/1 kg cape gooseberry juice
(about 4 lb 6 oz/2 kg whole fruit)
the juice of 1 lime
1½ cups/350 g white sugar
1⅔ cups/400 g brown sugar
1½ tsp agar-agar powder

Makes	*4–5 small jars*
Preparation time:	*15 minutes*
Resting time:	*1 hour*
Cooking time:	*25 minutes*
Difficulty:	*★*

Cape gooseberries, also called Chinese lanterns or physalis, are the fruit of a small bush cultivated in New Zealand. Nestled within a translucent papery orange hull is a golden amber, cherry-like fruit. The rich glow of the fruit gives the "lantern" its flame. If cape gooseberries are not available, ordinary gooseberries are a good substitute.

Cape gooseberries can be enjoyed just as they are or covered in chocolate, or even candied with fondant or caramel. They may also be used raw as a decorative garnish on pies and tarts. Cooked, they can be an accompaniment to venison or white meat, or are included in sweet and sour sauces, and often in preserves or jam as in this recipe.

Combining white and brown sugars gives this jelly a rich dark color without greatly changing the taste. All white sugar can be used if a lighter color is preferred.

For this jelly, once the jars have been filled with boiling jam, sealed and turned upside down, they should be left to cool. However, they must be turned upright again while still lukewarm; otherwise, the jelly will stick to the lid instead of sinking back down to the bottom of the jar.

For a striking presentation, serve this jelly in a bowl, garnished with one or two fresh whole cape gooseberries still in their papery hulls.

1. Remove the hulls from the chinese lanterns. Wash the fruit carefully, and pat dry.

2. Put the fruit through a blender or food processor, then strain through a sieve. Pour the strained juice into the preserving pan, then add the lime juice, white sugar, and brown sugar. Stir briskly. Let sit 1 hour.

Jelly

3. Bring the mixture to a boil and simmer for 25 minutes on high heat. Stir and skim regularly.

4. 5 minutes before the end of cooking, sprinkle the agar-agar powder on the jelly and stir thoroughly. While the jelly is still boiling, fill the sterilized jars, seal and turn upside down. When lukewarm, turn right side up again.

Chocolates and Candies

Tempering Chocolate

8¾ oz/250 g dark chocolate or
8¾ oz/250 g white chocolate or
8¾ oz/250 g milk chocolate

Makes: 60-70 pieces
Preparation time: 15 minutes
Difficulty: ★

Note the following "crystallization curve" guidelines, which are different for each type of chocolate.

For dark chocolate:
122°F–80.6°F–87.8°F/50°C–27°C–31°C

For milk chocolate:
113°F–80.6°F–84.2°F /45°C–27°C–29°C

For white chocolate:
113°F–80.6°F–82.4°F /45°C–27°C–28°C
(this also applies to red, green or yellow chocolate, which are white chocolate with coloring added)

In all its many forms—cocoa powder, chocolate bars or baking chocolate—chocolate remains the manna of romantics, symbolizing luxury and fine living. Its quality varies depending on the cocoa beans it is made from, the way it is processed, and the percentage of cocoa butter: Finer quality chocolate has more cocoa butter. For the following recipes, use chocolate with at least 50% cocoa butter. When buying white coating, read the label carefully. Inferior varieties lack cocoa butter entirely, and may not be labeled "chocolate."

Couverture chocolate for decorative finishes may be found in gourmet shops or candy supply stores. It can also be made by tempering high quality chocolate, whether dark, milk or white. Tempering involves heating chocolate, then cooling, then parti-

ally heating it again to stabilize the cocoa butter crystals and ensure a smooth shiny finish. Accurate temperatures are essential, so use a thermometer. Special chocolate tempering thermometers, more accurate at low temperatures than candy thermometers, are available at candy and baking supply stores.

If the chocolate coating is not shiny, the pan may be too damp, too cold, not the right temperature, or the chocolate may have cooled too long. Do not despair; simply remelt and re-temper the chocolate! But do not allow water to get in the melted chocolate, as this will ruining the coating.

White chocolates keep up to eight months, whereas milk chocolates can be kept for a year, and dark may last up to three years. Your homemade chocolates are sure to be a success!

1. Chop the chocolate into small pieces. Melt slowly in a double boiler until it reaches 113–122 °F/45–50 °C. (Temperatures are for dark chocolate. For milk or white chocolate, see the temperatures listed above.)

2. Pour half the melted chocolate out onto a cold work surface. A chilled marble slab is ideal.

for Coating

3. Using two metal spatulas, knead and scrape the melted chocolate on the cold work surface until the chocolate has cooled to 80.6 °F/27 °C.

4. Return the cooled, kneaded chocolate to the rest of the melted chocolate in the double boiler and stir, blending them together until the chocolate has reached 87.8 °F/31 °C. (Reheat the double boiler if necessary.) Dip the candies in the tempered chocolate, place them on wax paper, and let cool to room temperature (68 °F/20 °C).

Tropical Island

For the coconut truffles:
6½ tbsp/100 ml coconut milk
3½ oz/100 g white chocolate
scant 3 oz/80 g milk chocolate
2½ tbsp/20 g shredded coconut
1½ tbsp/20 g cocoa butter
6½ tbsp/100 ml coconut liqueur

For the pistachio truffles:
⅓ cup/70 ml fresh cream
scant 3 oz/80 g milk chocolate
2½ oz/70 g dark chocolate
1 oz/30 g pistachio paste
6½ tbsp/100 ml orange-flavored liqueur

For the papaya truffles:
6½ tbsp/100 ml papaya juice
scant 3 oz/80 g white chocolate
3½ oz/100 g milk chocolate
1½ tbsp/20 g cocoa butter
6½ tbsp/100 ml white rum

To finish:
10½ oz/300 g tempered dark chocolate
  (see p. 52)
1 generous cup/100 g shredded coconut
⅓ cup/50 g finely chopped pistachios
3½ tbsp/50 g white sugar
6½ tbsp/50 g unsweetened cocoa powder

Makes: 40 truffles
Preparation time: 1 hour
Difficulty: ★

Pleasure and good health needn't be mutually exclusive. These truffles are so rich and delicious that just a few mouthfuls satisfies your chocolate craving without breaking the calorie bank.

Coconut, pistachio and papaya are distinct variations on the tropical theme, but each truffle is made the same way. First, prepare a ganache by heating the liquid (coconut milk, fresh cream or papaya juice) and pouring it over the chocolate. Mix until smooth before adding the solid fat (cocoa butter or nut paste, which are available at gourmet shops or candy supply merchants). Liqueur is added last so the alcohol does not evaporate. The ganache is then rolled into balls and dipped in tempered chocolate. Finally, the truffles are rolled in coconut, chopped nuts, or sugar, and dusted with cocoa powder.

The same procedure may be used to invent other flavors of truffles. Marzipan and slivered almonds may be substituted for pistachio paste and chopped pistachios. Try mango juice or other exotic fruit juices instead of papaya juice. Mandarine Napoleon (tangerine-flavored), Amaretto (almond) or Frangelico (hazelnut) liqueur may be substituted for orange-flavored liqueur. The final coating, too, should complement the flavor of your truffles; for example, slivered almonds on truffles made with marzipan. A simple powdered-sugar coating goes well with any flavor. For a unique personal touch, sift a pinch of spice with the final coating of confectioners' sugar. A dash of ginger, cardamom, or curry powder will surprise and delight even the most jaded palates!

1. Make the coconut ganache by boiling the coconut milk, then pouring it onto the finely chopped chocolates. Add the shredded coconut and stir until thoroughly blended.

2. Melt the cocoa butter and, while it is still lukewarm, add it to the chocolate-coconut mixture. Pour in the coconut liqueur. Whisk briskly until very smooth.

Truffle Assortment

3. Set the ganache aside in a cool place (around 62.6 °F/17 °C) to thicken. When it has cooled enough to hold a shape, put the ganache in a pastry bag and squeeze bite-sized truffles onto wax paper. Dust your palms with unsweetened cocoa powder and roll the truffles between them to form nice round balls. Let the truffles set until firm.

4. Melt the dark chocolate until it reaches 87.8 °F/31 °C. Using a fork, dip the truffles in the melted chocolate, then roll them immediately in shredded coconut to finish. Make the pistachio and papaya truffles in the same way, varying the ingredients according to the text above.

Flamboyant

2½ cups/500 g sugar cubes
⅔ cup/150 ml water
6½ tbsp/100 ml glucose syrup
10 Szichuan peppercorns, finely ground
a few drops red food coloring
a few drops yellow food coloring

Makes:	*40 candies +*
	1 small "dish"
Preparation time:	*45 minutes*
Cooking time:	*5 minutes*
Difficulty:	★ ★ ★

These exotic-looking candies call for just a few ingredients, but require some care to make. It is extremely important to use proper tools and precautions when cooking with sugar! While sugar syrup boils at 212 °F, it can reach temperatures over 350 °F, and it not only burns but also sticks to the skin. For safety's sake, always use long-handled heatproof utensils and wear oven mitts or protective gloves.

Mixing bowls, too, should be heatproof and nonreactive; stainless steel or tempered glass are best. Sugar passes through different stages as it cooks, so an accurate candy or jelly thermometer is also essential. This recipe calls for glucose syrup, which is sold by candy supply specialists, but corn syrup may be substituted as follows: Bring two parts light corn syrup to a full boil. Remove it from heat, let it cool then add one part unheated corn syrup. Mix well. This should produce the right consistency with just a slightly different taste.

This candy can be made with many flavors: just add a drop of vanilla extract, bergamot, lemon, orange or mint... The color may also be changed to suit the flavor: green for mint or lime flavor, orange for mandarine, and so on.

Here is a simple technique to make pyramid shapes. Shape the candy into a long ⅜ in/1 cm diameter rod. Hold the rod in one hand and snip small pieces with scissors. Shift the angle of the scissors a quarter turn each time to create the distinctive pyramid shape.

For an artistic presentation, use part of the cooked sugar and some food color to shape a small "dish." Work quickly, as the candy is quite fragile once it cools.

1. Bring the sugar and water to a boil over high heat. When boiling, add the glucose. After it has cooked for about 5 minutes, add the ground peppercorns.

2. Check the temperature of the sugar often. When it reaches 320 °F/160 °C, carefully pour the boiling sugar mixture onto a cold, non-stick work surface, preferably marble. Pour out a circle for each different color.

Pyramids

3. Sprinkle a few drops of the desired food colorings onto the circles of hot candy. Blend in the color thoroughly, then quickly knead the mixture.

4. Roll the hot candy into long rods as shown, then use scissors to snip the rods into small pieces. Use any leftover candy mix to roll out and shape a leaf or dish. Leave to cool, then fill the "dish" with the pyramid-shaped candies.

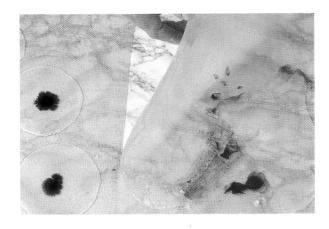

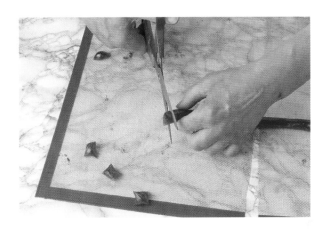

Dark Chocolate

For the caramel:
4½ oz/125 g semi-sweet chocolate
½ cup/125 g butter
5½ tbsp/125 ml honey
½ cup/125 g white sugar

For the coating:
2 oz/50 g tempered dark chocolate
¼ cup/30 g unsweetened cocoa

Makes:	*40 caramels*
Preparation time:	*20 minutes*
Cooking time:	*10 minutes*
Difficulty:	★

Like other recipes in this book, this one calls for the the best quality chocolate. Fine dark chocolate contains 55–75% cocoa butter, and displays reddish or mahogany highlights. Most chocolate makers use a blend of cocoa beans, but a few chocolatiers now produce fine chocolate, like fine wine, from a single type of bean. These rare and precious *grand cru* chocolates, made from such highly prized varieties as Venezuelan Criollo, are well worth searching out.

The honey in this recipe adds a subtle yet distinctive flavor that does not detract from the bittersweet taste of the chocolate. Different varieties of honey may be used, for instance acacia or lavender flower honey; but the assertive taste of pine honey does not suit these caramels.

The ingredients should be mixed in stages. First heat the butter, then the honey and melt them partially before adding the chocolate and sugar. This order of events prevents the caramel from sticking to the pan, which is important because even the slightest burning would cause an unpleasant bitter flavor. This is why, in any recipe involving cooked sugar, the pot must be watched constantly (despite the old saying)!

The edges and sides of the pan must also be kept clean during cooking. Use a pastry brush dipped in water to wipe away any sugar crystals that form. Otherwise these stray crystals will give the caramel a grainy texture, an odd taste, and a poor appearance.

This procedure guarantees perfect confections every time!

1. For the caramel, chop the semi-sweet chocolate into small pieces.

2. Melt the butter in a pot with the honey, then add the chocolate pieces and sugar. Bring to a boil and cook for about 10 minutes, stirring constantly until it has the consistency of medium-thick batter.

Caramels

3. To test for doneness, plunge a spoonful of the mixture into a pan of very cold water. If the caramel smudges slightly when you press a finger into it, it is ready.

4. Pour the caramel into a wax paper-lined cake pan. Set aside in a cool place (62.6 °F/17 °C) for 1 hour. Turn out of the cake pan in one piece. Reheat the tempered dark chocolate in a double boiler and spread a thin layer on the caramel. Then turn the caramel "cake" upside down and coat the other side. Sprinkle with unsweetened cocoa powder, and cut into small squares.

Coconut and

For the ganache:
6 oz/170 g milk chocolate
5 tbsp/75 ml heavy cream
¾ cup/75 g shredded coconut

For the coating:
½ cup/50 g shredded coconut
5¼ oz/150 g tempered dark or milk
chocolate

To serve (optional):
1 fresh coconut shell

Makes:	40 pieces
Preparation time:	25 minutes
Difficulty:	★

"Ganache" is the term for a rich blend of melted chocolate with milk, butter, or cream, plus a liquid flavoring. When soft, it may be spread and used as frosting. Shaped and set, it forms the basis of scrumptious candies like these.

The preparation of these little ganache "islands" is quite simple. First, half the ganache is spread into a block. When cooled, it is dipped in a fine layer of tempered dark or milk chocolate, which helps the candies retain their shape. The chocolate block is cut into strips, which are then halved to form triangles. Once the triangles have been cut, they are dipped individually in tempered chocolate, and placed on wax paper. They may then be decorated by lightly pressing the back of a fork onto the surface of each triangle, leaving a striped imprint.

The rest of the ganache is used to make round drops. These are also dipped individually in the tempered chocolate, which must be first warmed to about 85 °F/30 °C. A slight temperature variation of one or two degrees either way is acceptable.

For an elegant presentation highlighting the tropical theme, serve these chocolates in a unique "dish:" a fresh coconut shell broken open at one end. Sprinkle some white chocolate curls on top for contrast and texture. Or simply serve them on a pretty candy dish or small silver tray. Fine tea, coffee or liqueur is the perfect accompaniment for these delightful treats.

1. On a chopping board, cut the milk chocolate into small pieces using a very sharp, tapered knife.

2. Blend the cream and shredded coconut in a pot, and bring to a boil. Pour the boiled cream and coconut onto the milk chocolate pieces in a mixing bowl. Whisk thoroughly and set aside.

Chocolate Islands

3. When the mixture has cooled to about 62.6–68 °F/17–20 °C, form half of it into a block. Put the other half into a pastry bag and form round drops onto wax paper.

4. Reheat the tempered dark or milk chocolate in a double boiler, to about 85 °F/30 °C. Using a fork, dip the drops and triangles into the melted coating. Roll the drops in the shredded coconut. Let them cool, then arrange decoratively in a fresh coconut shell.

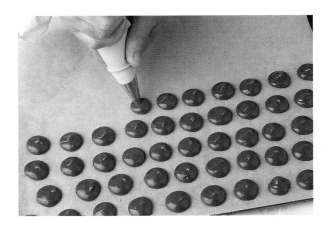

Dark Rum Pine

For the ganache:
scant 3 oz/80 g milk chocolate
scant 3 oz/80 g dark chocolate
⅓ cup/80 ml heavy cream
1½ tbsp/20 g butter
a few pink peppercorns, finely ground
2½ tbsp/40 g aged dark rum

To finish:
5¼ oz/150 g tempered dark chocolate
⅓ cup/50 g pine nuts

Makes: 40 chocolates
Preparation time: 25 minutes
Difficulty: ★

Even to a true chocolate lover, making homemade chocolates may seem time-consuming and intimidating. This recipe is especially designed to prove that making gourmet homemade chocolates can be easy and delicious.

The pine nuts should be roasted lightly in the oven to give them a slight crunch. Once they have cooled, they are used to decorate the chocolate balls. Lightly roasted pistachios, roasted slivered almonds, or a combination of nuts may be used for the same effect.

If time is not of the essence, create a base layer for each chocolate ball out of marzipan. Prepared marzipan paste is available in most supermarkets or gourmet shops. Roll out the marzipan to an even thickness, then use a small round cookie cutter to make circles. Lay the circles on wax paper and affix the chocolate balls to each with a few drops of melted chocolate dabbed onto the marzipan.

Orange-flavored liqueur may be substituted for the rum, and will add an exotic touch. Another delicious alternative is "Licor 43," an aromatic vanilla liqueur from Spain.

No one will be able to resist the sophisticated taste of these delectable chocolates!

1. Chop the milk and dark chocolate finely and set aside in a mixing bowl. Combine the cream, butter and ground pink pepper in a pot. Bring to a boil. Remove from the heat, add the rum, and blend well. Pour the hot mixture onto the chopped chocolate, stir to combine and set aside.

2. Put the chocolate mixture into a pastry bag and squeeze out chocolate balls onto wax paper. Lightly roast the pine nuts under the broiler, then let them cool.

Nut Chocolates

3. Finish shaping the chocolate balls by rolling them between your palms. Set aside to harden. Melt the tempered dark chocolate in a double boiler until it reaches 87.8 °F/31 °C. Using a fork, dip each ball into the melted chocolate, then place on wax paper.

4. Before the coated chocolate balls cool, lightly press a few toasted pine nuts on top of each. Let set in a cool place (about 63 °F/17 °C) before serving.

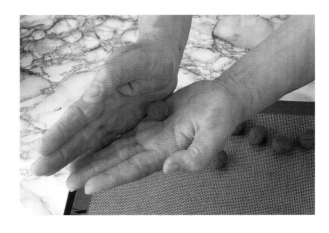

Mango-Licorice

For the ganache:
1 3-in/7-cm piece natural licorice root
5 tbsp/75 ml heavy cream
5 tbsp/75 ml mango juice
1½ tbsp/20 g butter
1 tbsp/15 g licorice powder
4¼ oz/120 g milk chocolate
2 oz/60 g dark chocolate

For the base layer:
3½ oz/100 g tempered dark chocolate

To finish:
1 tbsp/15 g white chocolate (optional)

Makes: 40 chocolates
Preparation time: 20 minutes
Difficulty: ★ ★

This recipe is an unusual and tempting blend of natural licorice and fine chocolate. Real licorice root may be purchased in health stores or by mail order, and is most often sold as a medicinal herb for its beneficial effects on the digestive and respiratory systems. It may be replaced by crushed aniseseed, but do not use fennel seed, which is too coarse for sweet dishes.

The mango juice adds a refreshing fruity tang. For variation, another tropical fruit juice may be substituted; for example, guava or papaya.

The best way to make these chocolates is to create a dark chocolate base layer, and place the ganache on top. For added interest, place small pieces of black licorice candy on the base layer before covering them with ganache.

The final decorative touch is a fine striped effect, achieved with a wax paper cone. First cut a large right triangle from the paper, then roll it into a cone. The wide end of the cone is then twisted closed, and the tip is snipped off with scissors leaving a small hole. Melt the white chocolate in a double boiler until it reaches 82.4 °F/28 °C. (If preferred, use milk or dark chocolate, melted to 84.2 °F/29 °C or 87.8 °F/31 °C respectively.) Half fill the cone with the melted chocolate, then squeeze it firmly and evenly. Draw fine lines of chocolate horizontally with a sweeping movement from side to side. This is essentially the same technique used in cake decorating.

1. Finely chop the licorice root into slivers. Reserve a teaspoon or two for garnish.

2. To make the ganache, combine the cream, mango juice, butter, chopped licorice and licorice powder in a pot. Bring to a boil. Chop the two kinds of chocolate and put in a mixing bowl, then pour the boiling cream mixture over the chocolate. Stir thoroughly and set aside.

Chocolates

3. For the base layer, melt the tempered dark chocolate in a double boiler until it reaches 87.8 °F/31° C. Fill a pastry bag or wax paper cone with the melted chocolate and squeeze onto wax paper 20 sets of three contiguous strips, ½ in/1.5 cm long, so that the three strips of chocolate spread into each other forming one band, as shown. Let cool until firm.

4. Fill a pastry bag with the ganache. Using a wide nozzle, squeeze a dollop of ganache onto each base. Melt the white chocolate in a double boiler until it reaches 82.4–84.2 °F/28–29 °C. Fill a pastry bag or wax paper cone with the white chocolate and decorate the candies with long, thin horizontal lines. Sprinkle the reserved licorice on top.

Spiced Honey

For the ganache:
6½ tbsp/100 ml heavy cream
2 tsp/10 g very finely ground coffee
1 tsp/5 g finely ground peppermill-blend
 pepper
2 tsp/10 g honey
scant 3 oz/80 g milk chocolate
1 oz/30 g dark chocolate

For the garnish:
2 tsp/10 g ground coffee

Makes: 35–40 chocolates
Preparation time: 25 minutes
Resting time 1 hour
Difficulty: ★

These voluptuous chocolates have a strong personality that will win over the most demanding gourmets. The combination of coffee and chocolate is perenially popular with chocolate lovers, and the originality of this recipe is in the presentation: chocolates in the shape of large coffee beans, as if they had come directly from an Ethiopian coffee plantation!

The four-pepper or peppermill-blend of white, green, pink and black peppercorns adds a surprising but perfect note of harmony to the coffee, a subtly heightened flavor sure to please the most discerning palates.

The ganache combines milk and dark chocolate, but it may be prepared with all dark chocolate for those who prefer a stronger, slightly bitter taste. In this case, however, the total

quantity should be reduced from four to three and one half ounces. If a pure milk chocolate ganache is preferred, the total quantity should be decreased by the same amount.

To put the finishing touch on these chocolates, after shaping them into coffee beans, sprinkle ground coffee or unsweetened cocoa powder on top. Different varieties of coffee may be used, to test the gourmets' palates! Chocolate-covered expresso beans may also be used as garnish.

The combination of chocolate and coffee is superb, and the particular charm of these mocha chocolates lies in the balance between the bitterness of each element and the smooth sweet richness of the ganache. Friends and family alike will devour these with gusto!

1. Heat the cream in a pot, sprinkle the very finely ground coffee on the cream and stir.

2. Add the finely ground pepper and honey and bring to a boil. Chop the milk and dark chocolate and add to the boiling mixture. Blend well and set aside in a mixing bowl.

Mocha Chocolates

3. Using a heatproof scraper, knead the ganache in the mixing bowl. Fill a pastry bag with the ganache.

4. Using a medium nozzle, squeeze balls of ganache onto a sheet of wax paper. With the tip of a knife, draw a deep line down the middle of each ball to make them look like coffee beans. Sprinkle the remaining ground coffee on top, then set the chocolates aside for 1 hour in a cool place (62.6 °F/17 °C) before serving.

Tropical

For the ganache:
6½ tbsp/100 ml heavy cream
⅛ tsp ground ginger
2 tsp/10 g ground star anise
⅛ tsp ground fennel
⅛ tsp black tea leaves
scant 3 oz/80 g milk chocolate
1 oz/30 g dark chocolate

For the "celestial circle":
1¾ oz/50 g tempered white chocolate
   (optional)
1¾ oz/50 g tempered milk chocolate
1¾ oz/50 g tempered dark chocolate

To finish:
1 pomegranate

Makes: 25 chocolates
Preparation time: 45 minutes
Difficulty: ★ ★ ★

Chocolate stars sparkle in a marbled sky in this dramatic, truly heavenly dessert. The "celestial circle" backdrop is not really difficult, but does require some care and patience. It is molded using a sheet of Rhodhoid; if this material is unavailable, heavy-duty shiny paper or plastic wrap may be substituted. The molding plastic must be cut out beforehand, and the tempered chocolates should be placed on it while still warm. They must be mixed with a spatula just enough to create a marbled effect, and then left to cool to the consistency of soft butter. The mold is then shaped into an arch by spreading it onto a rounded object like the bottom of an overturned bowl. If the object has a shiny surface, the marbled chocolate should also remain shiny. The

reverse is also true: if the object has a dull surface the marbled chocolate will be dull. The circle or bowl of marbled chocolate should be left to harden in a cool place before carefully removing the plastic backing sheet.

This manuever will be simpler if only one or two types of chocolate are used to make the marbled "circle." Only fine tempered chocolate should be used, not ordinary baking chocolate, which is of lesser quality.

The pomegranate seeds add a dash of color to this night sky. If unavailable, they may be replaced by other finely diced candied fruit, or by small red berries such as red currants or raspberries.

1. In a pot, boil the cream, then add the ginger, star anise, fennel and black tea. Meanwhile, melt each different type of tempered chocolate separately and set aside for making the "celestial circle."

2. Chop the milk and dark chocolate for the ganache and put it in a mixing bowl. Pour the boiled cream and spices over the chocolate, blend well and set aside. To make the "celestial circle" pour the melted tempered chocolates in random dollops on the molding sheet, spread, and use a spatula to mix for a marbled effect. Shape this marbled sheet of chocolate as desired and cool until firm.

Night Stars

3. To make the bases for the stars, place dime-sized flat dollops of melted dark chocolate onto a sheet of wax paper with a fingertip. Cool until firm. Reserve some melted chocolate to use as "glue" for sticking the stars onto the molded "celestial circle."

4. Put the ganache filling into a pastry bag with a star-shaped nozzle. Make 5-pointed stars on each base and place one pomegranate seed in the center of each star. Set the stars aside in a cool place until firm. Then "glue" each star to the "celestial circle" by placing a drop of melted dark chocolate on the marbled surface. Gently press each star onto the "glue."

Marbled

For the ganache filling:
2½ tbsp/40 ml mango juice
2½ tbsp/40 ml papaya juice
2½ tbsp/40 ml passion fruit juice
2½ tbsp/40 ml mandarine orange juice
2½ tbsp/40 ml pineapple juice
7 oz/200 g milk chocolate
5¼ oz/150 g white chocolate
1¾ oz/50 g dark chocolate
3½ tbsp/50 g butter

To finish:
10½ oz/300 g tempered milk chocolate
1 tbsp/10 g tempered white chocolate
1 tbsp/10 g tempered dark chocolate

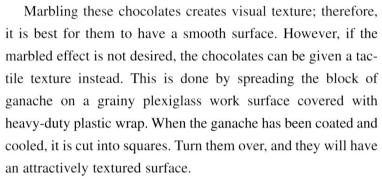

Makes:	60 chocolates
Preparation time:	45 minutes
Difficulty:	★ ★

Coating chocolate ganache with a thin outer layer of chocolate helps it retain its shape and makes it easier to cut and decorate. Certain precautions should be taken during the coating to ensure good results. Use a small fork to dip the candies into their chocolate coating. Then place each candy right side up so that any indentations left by the fork are hidden on the bottom.

An attractive finish can be created using Rhodoid or heavy-duty plastic wrap on chocolates that are covered with chopped dried fruit or unsweetened cocoa powder. First, cut squares of plastic wrap larger than the pieces of chocolate. Then press the squares firmly onto the top surface of the chocolates. This causes the fruit or cocoa to penetrate slightly, and when the plastic square is removed, the surface is smooth and shiny.

Marbling these chocolates creates visual texture; therefore, it is best for them to have a smooth surface. However, if the marbled effect is not desired, the chocolates can be given a tactile texture instead. This is done by spreading the block of ganache on a grainy plexiglass work surface covered with heavy-duty plastic wrap. When the ganache has been coated and cooled, it is cut into squares. Turn them over, and they will have an attractively textured surface.

A general rule of thumb when making chocolates is to be careful about the ambient humidity. If it is above 50%, the moisture in the air will affect the ganache, causing it to "seize" and harden.

1. Mix the fruit juices and boil them in a pot. Chop the 3 different types of chocolate for the ganache, and place in a mixing bowl. Pour the boiling fruit juices onto the chocolate, stir, add the butter, and blend well. Set aside to cool at room temperature (62.6–68 °F/17–20 °C).

2. Blend the ganache and spread it in a cake pan or on a plexiglass board lined with heavy-duty plastic wrap. Let it harden, then remove from the cake pan. In a double boiler, melt the milk chocolate for the finishing coating until it reaches 84.2 °F/29 °C. Using a spatula, cover the ganache block with some of the melted chocolate. Heat the knife blade before cutting the block into squares.

Island Delights

3. Dip each square into the remaining melted chocolate and place on wax paper. Before the squares harden completely, melt the tempered dark and white chocolate separately. Use 2 paper cones as pastry bags to squeeze 2 small dollops, one of dark and one of white chocolate, onto each square, just touching the square with the tip of the cone to lightly press the dollop into the soft milk chocolate layer.

4. Spread with a knife tip or fork tines to marble the surface of each square. Cut squares of plastic about twice the size of the chocolate squares. Place a plastic square on each chocolate, pressing lightly with a fingertip to even the surface. Allow the squares to cool, then remove the plastic.

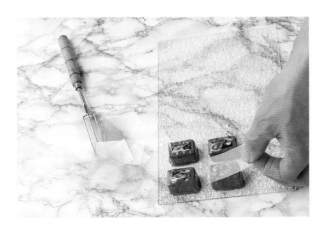

Piña Colada

For the pineapple-coconut ganache:
2½ tbsp/40 ml coconut milk
generous ⅓ cup/60 g pineapple chunks, cut
 into small pieces
2 tbsp/30 g butter
scant 3 oz/80 g dark chocolate
scant 3 oz/80 g white chocolate
2 tsp/10 ml dark rum

To finish:
5¼ oz/150 g tempered dark chocolate
6½ tbsp/50 g unsweetened cocoa powder

Makes: 35–40 chocolates
Preparation time: 35 minutes
Difficulty: ★ ★

These exotic chocolates combine the same ingredients as the not-so-secret formula of the famous cocktail, Piña Colada, in an unusual way. Pineapple, coconut and rum remain the basic trio, but combined with chocolate they make a deliciously harmonious quartet.

Success is guaranteed if the basic instructions are carefully followed. Most important in this recipe is observing the order in which the ingredients are added. First, the boiling coconut milk-pineapple mixture must be poured onto the chopped chocolate. If the chocolate is added to the boiling liquid, the casein or milk proteins contained in the chocolate could produce an unpleasant smell. The rum should be added at the end, otherwise the alcohol would evaporate too early, and its rich flavor would be lost. Those who prefer not to use alcohol can replace the rum with the same quantity of pineapple juice, coconut juice or non-alcoholic rum-flavored extract.

The easiest way to form these chocolates is to simply shape the ganache into balls, but it can also be poured into molds, for example, cookie cutters placed on a sheet of wax paper or heavy plastic wrap. Let the ganache rest until completely firm before removing the mold.

Another way to decorate these chocolates elegantly is to use a warm metal stamp or punch to make an imprint of a heart, star, clover leaf or other design on the surface of each chocolate. Let your imagination be your guide!

1. Combine the coconut milk and the small pineapple chunks in a pot over high heat. Add the butter.

2. Chop the white and dark chocolate for the ganache and place in a mixing bowl. Pour the hot coconut-milk mixture over the chocolate and stir until melted.

Chocolates

3. Add the rum to the ganache, blend well, and set aside in a cool place (62.6 °F/17 °C) for about 15 minutes. Shape the ganache into balls and place them on a sheet of wax paper. Set aside for another 15 minutes, or until firm.

4. To finish, dust your hands with unsweetened cocoa powder, dip the balls in a dish of cocoa powder and roll the balls in your palms. Melt the tempered dark chocolate in a double boiler until it reaches 87.8 °F/31 °C. Using a fork, dip the balls in the coating, dust with cocoa powder again, and place on wax paper to cool.

White Chocolate

For the caramel:
2 tbsp/30 ml lime juice
1¼ cups/300 g white sugar
5 tbsp/75 g cold butter
5 tbsp/75 g cocoa butter
the rind of 1 lime, grated
scant 8 oz/220 g white chocolate

To finish:
1 tbsp/10 g tempered dark chocolate

Makes:	40–50 caramels
Preparation time:	15 minutes
Resting time:	1 hour
Cooking time:	15 minutes
Difficulty:	★

Small amounts of chocolate can be melted in the microwave, preferably in glass containers, with the oven set to medium power. Watch the chocolate closely, checking every 30 seconds. It should only take a minute or two, depending on the power of the oven. The chocolate will appear to retain some of its shape, but upon stirring it will melt and blend together. Be careful! Just a few seconds too long in the microwave will ruin the chocolate. This method works best with dark chocolate, moderately well with milk and white chocolate, and is not suitable for the tempering process, which requires controlled temperatures.

The counterpoint of sweet white chocolate and tangy lime makes this recipe extra special. To achieve just the right texture, the caramel must not be heated above 244 °F/118 °C. The combination of butter, cocoa butter and white chocolate makes these candies quite rich, so they will not become very hard. The higher the quality of the ingredients, the longer the caramels will keep. They should be individually wrapped with plastic wrap to preserve their soft, creamy consistency and stored in an airtight container at room temperature.

Other flavors may be substituted for the lime juice; for example, pineapple or any citrus fruit juice would taste lovely.

The decorative dark chocolate garnishes should be small and delicate so as not to affect the taste of the caramel. To make an impromptu pastry bag for decorating, fill a small plastic sandwich bag with the melted chocolate, snip off one corner, and squeeze. Voila!

1. Combine the lime juice, sugar, butter, cocoa butter and grated lime rind in a pot. Cook until the mixture reaches 244.4 °F/118 °C, about 15 minutes.

2. Chop the white chocolate and place it in a mixing bowl. Pour the cooked mixture over it and stir thoroughly.

Lime Caramels

3. Cover a cake pan or mold with plastic wrap, pour the mixture into the mold, and set aside for 1 hour.

4. Unmold the caramel in one block onto a wax paper-covered cutting board. Remove the plastic wrap, dip a large knife in hot water and cut the caramel into squares, wiping the blade and dipping in hot water between each cut. To finish, melt the tempered dark chocolate in a double boiler until it reaches 87.8 °F/31 °C. Fill a small paper cone or pastry bag with the dark chocolate and decorate the squares.

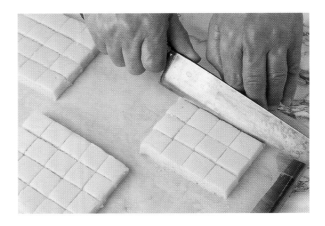

For the ganache:
3½ oz/100 g milk chocolate
scant 3 oz/80 g white chocolate
6½ tbsp/100 ml mango juice
a pinch freshly ground white pepper
1½ tbsp/20 g cocoa butter
2 tsp/10 ml lychee liqueur

For the base layer:
3½ oz/100 g tempered dark chocolate

To finish:
1 small jar mango jelly
1 small jar pineapple jelly
1 small jar kiwi jelly
1 small jar banana jelly
1 tsp/5 ml grenadine syrup

Makes: 30 chocolates
Preparation time: 45 minutes
Difficulty: ★

These chocolate "jewels" taste quite extraordinary thanks to their contrasting but complementary flavors. They are sure to surprise and delight with their innovative mixture of fruit flavored chocolate and tropical fruit jellies, and their artistic presentation. The four different jellies were chosen for their variety of bright colors; they will look fabulous together on a serving tray. But there is such a range of exotic jellies available that any number of flavors and colors can be used. Be as creative as you like!

The dark chocolate bases provide a sturdy bottom layer to hold these jewels together. If preferred, the base layer could be made from milk or white chocolate instead. The fruit juice and liqueur used to make the ganache may likewise be varied, provided that the proportions of liquid and chocolate are respected, and the same procedure is followed.

The pinch of white pepper adds a spicy note to the mango juice and chocolate. Other types of pepper should not be substituted, as they would risk dominating the delicate fruity flavor of the ganache.

These chocolates may be kept for approximately two weeks at room temperature (62.6–68 °F/17–20 °C).

1. Chop the chocolate to be used for the ganache and place in a mixing bowl. In a pan, bring the mango juice and pepper to a boil, then pour over the chocolate and stir. Melt the cocoa butter and let it cool slightly, then add it to the mango-chocolate mix while still warm. Stir in the lychee liqueur, mix well and set aside.

2. To make the bases, melt the tempered dark chocolate in a double boiler until it reaches 87.8 °F/31 °C. Fill a pastry bag or paper cone with the melted chocolate, and squeeze dime-sized dollops onto a baking sheet lined with wax paper. Tap the baking sheet gently to help the dollops flatten and spread evenly. Let cool.

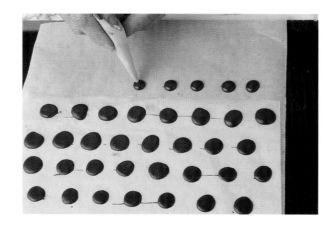

Fruit Jewels

3. Fill a pastry bag tipped with a small nozzle with the ganache, and squeeze spirals around the outside edge of each base, leaving a hole in the middle. Let these harden. Make paper cones for each type of jelly. Add a few drops of grenadine syrup to the mango jelly.

4. Fill each cone with jelly, snip off the tip and carefully squeeze out a dollop of jelly to fill each chocolate case.

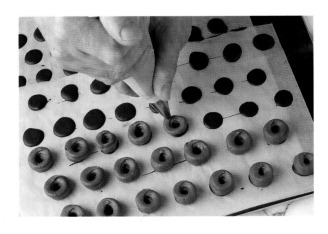

Jasmine-Star

For the candied fruit:
2 perfect star fruits
the juice of 1 lime
2 tbsp/30 g white sugar

For the sugar syrup:
   (see basic recipe)
6½ tbsp/100 g white sugar
3½ tbsp/50 ml water

Makes: 25 chocolates
Preparation time: 15 minutes
Difficulty: ★

For the ganache:
⅓ cup/80 ml heavy cream
⅓ cup/70 ml star fruit juice
1 tbsp/15 g jasmine tea leaves
3½ oz/100 g milk chocolate
2 oz/60 g dark chocolate

For the decoration:
a few dried currants (optional)
confectioners' sugar or cocoa powder
   (optional)

With the heady scent of jasmine flowers filling the air, these chocolates will transport you to the islands! No other flower could begin to perfume chocolate ganache the way jasmine can, and the exotic scent combines perfectly with the slight tanginess of the star fruit juice. star fruit, or carambola, were chosen for their beautiful shape, and because they remain firm and crunchy when candied.

Other exotic fuits also combine well with jasmine; for example, mango or cherimoya juice may be substituted for the star fruit, and slices of mango may be used for the presentation. In this case, however, the mango slices should not be candied.

Some cherimoya seeds may be used as decoration, strategically placed around the chocolates on the serving dish.

Whatever the choice of fruit, it should be of best quality. Star fruit should be ripe, but still firm, without the slightest blemish. Once sliced, they should be sprinkled with lime juice to prevent them from turning black when they come in contact with the air.

Chocolate chips may be used in place of the dried currants to garnish these chocolate stars. Powdered or superfine sugar and unsweetened cocoa powder dusted on the plate make a professional finishing touch.

1. To candy the fruit, slice the star fruit as shown, remove the seeds, sprinkle with lime juice, and set aside to be used as the base layer for the chocolates. Make the sugar syrup by combining the sugar and water. Bring to a boil, and cook until it reaches 215–219 °F/102–104 °C according to a candy thermometer. At this stage, the syrup should drip from the edge of a spoon in a thin thread.

2. As soon as the syrup has cooled to 104 °F/40 °C, dip each star fruit slice into the syrup on one side only, then dip the slice into the superfine sugar, and place on paper towel to dry.

Fruit Chocolates

3. Continue with all the star fruit slices. For the ganache, combine the cream and star fruit juice in a pot, heat, add the jasmine tea leaves and bring to a boil. Chop up the milk and dark chocolate and place it in a mixing bowl.

4. Pour the boiling mixture over the chopped chocolate, stir and set aside for 15 minutes in a cool place place (62.6 °F/17 °C). Place the fruit stars on an elegant serving plate. Then fill a pastry bag with the ganache and squeeze a mound onto each candied star. Garnish each mound with a dried currant. Dust the plate with sugar and cocoa powder, and serve.

Oriental

For the ganache:
5 fresh mint leaves
2 tsp/10 g dried mint tea leaves
⅔ cup/150 ml heavy cream
5 white pepper corns, freshly ground
4 oz/120 g milk chocolate
1¾ oz/50 g dark chocolate

For the sugar syrup:
(see basic recipe)
2 cups plus 1 tbsp/500 g white sugar
1 cup/250 ml water

For the decoration:
a few kumquats
1½ oz/40 g tempered white chocolate
7 fresh mint leaves

Serves — 4
Preparation time: — 35 minutes
Difficulty: — ★ ★

There is a story dating back to the 19th century about a baker's apprentice who accidentally spilled liquid into melted chocolate. In those days, chocolate was an expensive luxury, so the baker scolded the lad, but could not throw away the chocolate. Instead, he mixed the two ingredients, and discovered a "must" in every chocolate-maker's repertoire: ganache!

The unusual ganache in this recipe is made with a unique combination of spices. The ground pepper adds piquancy to the chocolate while the mint makes it cool and refreshing, and the tea perfumes it deliciously. Those who enjoy spicy food may increase the amounts of these ingredients to taste.

The fine texture of the ganache depends essentially on the quality of the chocolate, which in turn depends on the percen-tage of cocoa butter it contains. This should be about 70% for dark chocolate. For white or milk chocolate, the cocoa butter content should be the highest available.

For the sugar syrup to be just right, it should be cooked to the correct stage and then cooled just until it reaches the ideal temperature of 98.6–104 °F/37–40 °C before the fresh mint leaves are dipped in it. Then immediately dredge the coated mint leaves in white sugar to ensure they retain their vibrant green color. The mint leaves may be candied the day before making the ganache, or even several days or weeks ahead. They keep perfectly stored in an airtight container in a cool dry place.

1. Finely slice the kumquats for the decoration and set them aside. Remove the central vein from each of the 5 mint leaves for the ganache.

2. Crush the tea leaves with the flat side of a knife blade. Chop and crush the deveined mint leaves. Combine the cream, crushed tea leaves and mint leaves in a pot, and bring to a boil. Add the ground pepper. Chop the milk and dark chocolate and place in a mixing bowl. Pour the boiling mixture over the chocolate, stir, and set aside in a cool place (59–64.4 °F/ 15–18 °C).

Ganache

3. For the decoration, chop the white chocolate very finely. Melt it in a double boiler and hold at a temperature of 80.6–82.4 °F/27–28 °C. Using a pastry brush, paint the entire surface of a small plate with the melted white chocolate. Cool until firm. Make the sugar syrup by combining the sugar and water in a pot. Boil the syrup, then allow it to cool to 98.6–104 °F/ 37–40 °C.

4. Using tweezers and fingertips, dip the upper side of each of the 7 mint leaves for the garnish into the syrup, so that just the top and the edges are coated, then in sugar. Place the leaves decoratively on the white chocolate-covered plate. Fill a pastry bag with the ganache and squeeze decorative dollops onto the mint leaves and the center of the plate. Garnish with sliced kumquat.

Cherimoya

For the ganache:
generous ⅓ cup/60 g cherimoya flesh
¼ cup/60 ml heavy cream
a pinch white pepper
the juice of ½ a lime
2 oz/60 g white chocolate
6 tbsp/90 g cocoa butter, melted

For the coating:
1 tbsp/10 g tempered dark chocolate
1¾ oz/50 g tempered white chocolate

Makes: *40 chocolates*
Preparation time: *30 minutes*
Difficulty: ★

There are a thousand and one ways to savor life's joys, and chocolate is one of the best: a natural accompaniment to the convivial atmosphere around a dinner table. These unique, voluptuous candies combine exotic cherimoya with the sensuous richness of white chocolate.

The cherimoya has a creamy white flesh that blends perfectly with the color and flavor of white chocolate. In this recipe, pristine squares are laced with a delicate perfume and a hint of tropical spice. White pepper, sometimes called "confectioners' salt," is essential to this confection because it subtly enhances and balances the other flavors. Other types of pepper should be avoided, however, as their color would mar these pure white squares. The only exception would be a dash of black pepper, added inconspicuously to the dark chocolate for the decoration.

Molding frames are available from gourmet cookware stores or candy supply merchants. They may also be simply made by gluing or tacking together 4 strips of heavy cardboard or light plywood, about an inch wide, to form a square.

These creamy confections may be enjoyed with a glass of chilled champagne or a cup of hot tea, but always with friends. As they say in France: "Chocolate is a gift to be shared."

1. Peel the cherimoya and remove the seeds. Purée the flesh in a blender or food processor with the cream.

2. In a pot, combine this mixture with the ground white pepper and lime juice. Bring to a boil. Chop the white chocolate finely and place in a mixing bowl. Pour the boiling mixture over the chocolate, then add the melted cocoa butter and stir.

Ganache

3. Cover a baking sheet with plastic wrap or wax paper, and place a bottomless frame on top. Pour the ganache into the frame and smooth the surface with a spatula until the frame is evenly filled. Set aside in a cool place (62.6–64.4 °F/17–18 °C) until firm.

4. Unmold the block of ganache. Melt the white chocolate for the decoration in a double boiler, and nap the surface of the ganache block. Slice the block into small squares. Melt the tempered dark chocolate and decorate the squares. As soon as the squares are ready, place them on a sheet of plastic wrap and store.

For the spicy ganache:
6½ tbsp/100 ml heavy cream
1 tsp/5 g ground ginger
3½ oz/100 g dark chocolate
1¾ oz/50 g milk chocolate
2 tbsp/20 g finely chopped candied ginger
2 tbsp/20 g finely crushed almond brittle

For the almond brittle:
¾ cup/150 g white sugar
6½ tbsp/100 ml glucose syrup
1 cup/125 g slivered or chopped almonds

For the coating:
2 tbsp/20 g finely crushed almond brittle
2 tbsp/20 g chopped green pistachios
2 tsp/10 g pink pepper
8¾ oz/250 g tempered dark chocolate

Makes: 40–45 chocolates
Preparation time: 40 minutes
Difficulty: ★

The combination of crunchy almond brittle and chewy candied ginger gives these chocolates a pleasant texture and a burst of flavor. For those who find ginger a little too spicy, a pinch of ground star anise or cinnamon may be used instead, accompanied by two tablespoons of chopped candied fruit.

For best results in this recipe, the almond brittle should be homemade. To make it, the glucose should be heated but not boiled over moderate heat. Next the sugar is added and heated until the mixture begins to caramelize and turn golden brown. Be careful that the caramel does not scorch. Add the chopped or slivered almonds, blend well, and immediately pour it onto a

baking sheet covered with plastic wrap. The candy is then covered with another sheet of plastic wrap, spread evenly with a rolling pin, and left to cool. The almond brittle may be prepared a day or two ahead of time and stored in an airtight container at room temperature.

Although delicious coated simply in dark chocolate, for an artistic presentation and delicious variation, dip some of the ganache logs in melted white or milk chocolate.

These refined and dainty morsels will be greatly appreciated by all chocolate lovers.

1. Prepare the almond brittle as described in the text above. To make the ganache, combine the cream and ground ginger in a pot and bring to a boil. Chop the chocolate and place it in a mixing bowl. Pour the boiling cream over the chocolate.

2. Add the finely chopped candied ginger and crushed almond brittle, blend well and set aside. For the coating, crush 2 tbsp/20 g more of the almond brittle, chop the pistachios finely, and grind the pepper. Mix all 3 and set aside.

Spice Logs

3. Blend the cooled ganache with a spatula, place it in a pastry bag, and squeeze thick logs onto a sheet of wax paper. Set aside in a cool place (62.6 °F/17 °C) for about 15–20 minutes until firm.

4. For the coating, melt the tempered dark chocolate in a double boiler until it reaches 87.8 °F/31 °C. With a fork, dip each ganache log into the melted chocoalte, then roll in the pistachio-almond brittle-pepper mixture until completely coated. Place on a serving dish and set aside until firm.

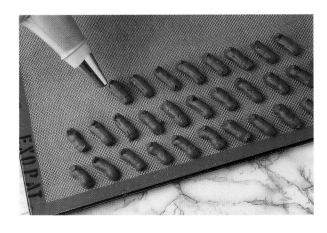

Jellied

For the fruit paste:
2 whole pomegranates or 3 cups/750 ml
  pomegranate juice
2¼ cups/550 g white sugar
2 tsp/10 g butter
the juice of 1 lemon
3½ tbsp/50 g pectin

For the decoration:
6½ tbsp/100 g coarse sugar
a few fresh mint leaves (optional)

Serves   *4*
Preparation time: *20 minutes*
Cooking time: *a few minutes*
Chilling time: *24 hours*
Difficulty: ★ ★

The pomegranate is considered a symbol of love and fertility because of its brilliant red color, round shape and multitude of seeds. According to the Greek myth of Persephone, the seeds of the pomegranate are responsible for the seasons of the year. Pomegranates are rich in phosphorus and in pectin, so they are perfect for making jellied fruit. The pectin called for in the ingredients may be replaced by an equivalent amount of dried, granulated gelatin. Whole pomegranates are in season around Christmas time, when their festive color is a traditional addition to many holiday tables; if they are unavailable, look for bottled pomegranate juice in Middle Eastern markets.

Making jellied fruit is rather like making jam, except that the final texture is dry and firm. If the following procedure is carefully followed, then any red fruit—such as strawberries, red currants or raspberries—may be used in place of pomegranate. Citrus fruit may also be substituted, but in this case the fruit should be heated for 20 seconds on high in a microwave. This trick allows the maximum of juice to be extracted. The jellied fruit will keep for a long time at room temperature as long as some moisture is retained.

To finish, the jellied fruit is rolled in coarse sugar. Thin strips of the rind from the same fruit may be used to garnish the serving plate. Cut into decorative shapes, this fruit makes a brilliant, colorful end to a dinner party.

1. Peel the pomegranates and cut them in chunks. Put through a blender, food mill or processor, then strain. Boil the juice in a pot with 2 cups/500 g sugar, the butter and lemon juice.

2. Combine the remaining sugar with the pectin, and add to the boiled juice. Stir and boil for another 2 minutes. Then pour the mixture out onto a large baking sheet.

Pomegranate

3. Refrigerate the jelly overnight. The next day, use a cookie cutter to cut shapes in the jellied fruit.

4. Dip each piece into coarse sugar, coat well, and place on a serving dish. Garnish with the mint leaves.

Chinese Lantern

For the ganache:
5 tbsp/75 ml heavy cream
a pinch of ground green pepper
a pinch of ground black pepper
5 tbsp/75 ml dark rum
3½ oz/100 g dark chocolate
1¾ oz/50 g white chocolate
20 cape gooseberries

Makes: 20 chocolates
Preparation time: 40 minutes
Difficulty: ★ ★

These exquisite chocolates are so easily made that they can be whipped up for unexpected guests or a special occasion on a moment's notice. The two different types of pepper are the key ingredient in this unique confection, to bring out the flavor of the two different chocolates.

The papery skin of cape gooseberries resembles Chinese lanterns and makes them a particularly beautiful choice, but cherries or grapes can be used, or even dried fruit such as figs, dates, or large raisins. Dark rum was chosen to smooth and round out the ganache in this recipe, but other alcohol may be successfully substituted, especially orange-flavored liqueurs.

For a non-alcoholic version, substitute the same quantity of orange or pineapple juice.

Remember that there is a precise temperature sequence to be followed when tempering the chocolate. First, the chocolate should be melted to 122 °F/50 °C, then cooled to 80.6 °F/27 °C by pouring half onto a cold marble work surface before mixing it back in with the other half. Finally, the chocolate is reheated in a double boiler until it reaches 87.8 °F/31 °C. It must be kept warm throughout the coating process. This is the key to success in making perfectly finished chocolates.

1. Boil the cream and 2 types of pepper in a pot. Remove from the heat and add the rum. Reserve half of the dark chocolate for the finishing coat. Finely chop the rest of the dark and white chocolate and place in a mixing bowl. Pour on the boiling cream, combine well and set aside.

2. Temper the reserved dark chocolate and hold warm. Cut 20 squares of aluminum foil, 3¼ x 3¼ in/8 x 8 cm. Wrap a square around the end of a thick stick (about ¾ in/2 cm in diameter), and dip the end of the stick in the warm chocolate. Carefully remove the dipped foil, place on a plate and wrap the next square around the end of the stick. Continue this way until all the chocolate bases are made. Set aside to cool and harden.

Chocolates in a Jewel Case

3. Hold the cape gooseberries between finger and thumb and carefully pull the papery hull away from the fruit without removing it. Then, holding each lantern by the hull, dip the fruit into the melted chocolate. Remove and let drip, then place on a sheet of wax paper to cool until firm.

4. Carefully remove the aluminum foil squares from the chocolate bases. Fill a pastry bag with the ganache, and squeeze a dollop into each chocolate base. Allow to harden a little, then press a chocolate-covered fruit into each case, hull or stem end up. Arrange elegantly on a serving dish.

Melon

For the ganache:
¾ cup/150 g peeled, seeded cantaloupe
2 tbsp/30 ml dark rum
2 tsp/10 ml lime juice
6½ tbsp/100 g cocoa butter
3½ oz/100 g white chocolate

For the bases:
1¾ oz/50 g white chocolate

For the decoration:
a few milk chocolate curls
3½ oz /100 g tempered dark chocolate

Makes:	40 chocolates
Preparation time:	25 minutes
Chilling time:	10 minutes
Difficulty:	★

Candy-making is like *haute couture*: The advice of the masters must be followed to reach the height of the art. Fortunately, the artistic presentation of these chocolates is much easier to create than it appears. The key to success is simply to leave the chocolate-covered dish in the refrigerator for ten minutes, to ensure that it will hold its shape.

A more elaborate backdrop may be created by using two or three different tempered chocolates, spread on a sheet of heavy-duty plastic wrap or a plastic mold, and mixed for a marbled effect. Different chocolates may also be used for the chocolate curls or shavings, which are made by scraping a piece of chocolate with a very sharp knife or vegetable peeler.

The cantaloupe may be replaced with another sweet, fleshy fruit such as honeydew melon, cassava, watermelon, kiwi, or papaya; however, citrus fruit should be avoided, as it is too acid for this ganache.

To decorate the ganache balls, fill a paper cone or pastry bag with melted chocolate and draw long lines back and forth over the whole baking sheet. Allow to cool and harden before lifting the chocolates off the sheet.

This beautiful dessert is the perfect finish for a romantic, gourmet *tête-à-tête*.

1. Blend the melon with the rum and lime juice in a blender or food processor. Pour into a pot and bring to a boil.

2. Melt the cocoa butter in a double boiler. Chop the white chocolate for the ganache and add to the cocoa butter. Stir. Add the hot fruit mixture and blend well. To make the bases, melt the white chocolate in a double boiler until it reaches 82.4 °F/28 °C. Dip a finger into the melted chocolate and dab onto a sheet of wax paper; repeat to make about 40 "penny" bases. Cool until firm.

Ganache

3. Melt the dark chocolate in a double boiler until it reaches 87.8°F/31°C. Use a pastry brush to paint the melted chocolate onto the bottom of an elegant dish. Refrigerate 10 minutes, or until firm. When the melon ganache has the consistency of soft butter, put it in a pastry bag, and squeeze a ball onto each white chocolate base.

4. Decorate each ball with thin lines of melted dark chocolate using a paper cone or pastry bag. Then "glue" each ganache ball onto the chocolate-covered serving dish with a drop of melted chocolate. Garnish with milk chocolate curls or shavings, and store in a cool place until serving time.

Praline

For the praline balls:
generous ½ cup/130 g cane sugar
1 cup/130 g whole hazelnuts
   or scant 1½ cups/130 g shredded coconut
   or ¾ cup/130 g dried papaya
2 oz/60 g milk chocolate

To finish:
1 oz/30 g tempered milk chocolate
1 oz/30 g tempered dark chocolate
generous ⅓ cup/50 g finely chopped
   almonds, lightly roasted

Makes:	*30 balls*
Preparation time:	*35 minutes*
Cooking time:	*10 minutes*
Difficulty:	*★*

These are everybody's favorite, classic praline-covered chocolate balls! Most people succumb very quickly to this temptation.

This recipe gives three variations on the praline theme: milk chocolates rolled in toasted, chopped almonds; milk chocolates rolled in crushed hazelnut praline, and dipped again in milk chocolate; and finally, dark chocolates rolled in crushed hazelnut praline and then dipped in dark chocolate.

Adventurous cooks can vary the flavor of the chocolates with exotic fruits and spices, for example, ground cinnamon.

Shredded coconut or dried papaya may be marinated in orange-flavored liqueur or another favorite, then added to the chocolate. Or add finely chopped raisins or ground coffee to make up part of the total amount of nuts.

This recipe is easy to make but requires a bit of time and patience. For convenience, the nut praline may be made ahead of time. These chocolates can also be made when time is available, and stored in an airtight container at a cool room temperature (62.6–68 °F/17–20 °C) until needed.

1. Make hazelnut praline with the sugar and nuts (see basic recipe). Cool and crush or grind it to pieces the size of peppercorns, and set ⅓ aside. Melt the milk chocolate in a double boiler to 84.2 °F/29 °C and stir in the rest of the praline. Put in a pastry bag and squeeze the chocolate into long, thick rods. Let harden slightly, then cut into short pieces. Roll each piece into a ball.

2. For the coating, melt the tempered milk chocolate in a double boiler. Put a spoonful in your palm, and roll a ball around your palm until covered with milk chocolate. Coat all the balls this way.

Balls

3. Roll ⅓ of the balls in the remaining crushed hazelnut brittle, then coat again with melted milk chocolate. Roll another ⅓ of the balls in the lightly roasted chopped almonds.

4. Melt the tempered dark chocolate in a double boiler until it reaches 87.8 °F/31 °C. Coat the remaining balls with the dark chocolate, then roll in the crushed hazelnut brittle. Dip again in the dark chocolate. Place all the praline balls on a sheet of wax paper to cool until fim.

Safari

For the almond praline:
½ cup/100 g brown sugar
⅔ cup/100 g almonds

For the coating:
2 oz/60 g tempered milk chocolate

For the decoration:
5¼ oz/150 g tempered dark chocolate
1¾ oz/50 g tempered white chocolate

Makes: 25 chocolates
Preparation time: 1 hour
Cooking time: 10 minutes
Difficulty: ★ ★

The almonds for the praline, or brittle, in this recipe should be of high quality, and should be caramelized by cooking with the brown sugar in a copper or stainless steel pot. Once cooled, the praline should be ground as finely as possible. The milk chocolate should be chopped, then melted in a double boiler until it reaches 84.2 °F/29 °C. The ground almond brittle is then blended with the melted chocolate.

The soft chocolate-praline mixture is poured into a bottomless frame and set on a work surface that has been covered with plastic wrap to prevent sticking. This block of chocolate is then left to cool and harden at a cool room temperature (62.6–68 °F/17–20 °C) before being cut into squares.

Homemade praline tastes best and may be made ahead to save time. Or, for convenience, store-bought praline may be used, freeing more time to make the "zebra stripe" decoration which gives these chocolates their distinctive "safari" allure.

The zebra stripes are easy to make with a clean plastic cake comb. A "comb" may be created by using scissors to cut "teeth" into the edge of a heavy-duty plastic square; the size and width of the teeth can thus be custom-designed.

The stripes may also be reversed, that is, white chocolate may be used to coat the squares and dark chocolate for the zebra effect. An elegant final touch would be to garnish each coated square with a whole almond.

1. To make the almond praline, combine the brown sugar and whole almonds in a heavy-bottomed pot and cook until caramelized (around 10 minutes). Check to see if the ideal stage has been reached by cutting one almond in half to see if the inside has turned brown.

2. Let the almond brittle cool, then finely grind in a blender or food processor. Make the chocolate squares as described in the text above.

Chocolates

3. For the zebra stripes, melt the white chocolate in a double boiler until it reaches 82.4 °F/28 °C. Spread it thinly on a sheet of heavy-duty plastic wrap. Then scrape a comb through it to create straight zebra stripes. Set aside to cool and harden at room temperature (62.6–68 °F/17–20 °C).

4. Melt the dark chocolate in a double boiler until it reaches 87.8 °F/31 °C. Use a fork to dip the cooled praline squares into the melted dark chocolate. Place the squares on the white chocolate stripes so that the pattern is diagonal, and press lightly with the fork. Set aside to harden. Finally, cut around the edges of each square with a knife, lift off the plastic wrap, and place each chocolate striped side up on a serving platter.

Marbled

For the hazelnut praline ganache:
⅔ cup/100 g hazelnuts
½ cup/100 g brown sugar
2 oz/60 g milk chocolate

For the garnish:
generous 2 tbsp/30 g candied orange peel
generous 2 tbsp/30 g candied citron

To finish:
1 oz/30 g tempered milk chocolate
1 oz/30 g tempered dark chocolate

Makes: 30 squares
Preparation time: 45 minutes
Cooking time: a few minutes
Difficulty: ★ ★

These luscious ganache squares combine a rich palette of flavors, from the sweet-sour bite of candied citrus to the smooth richness of chocolate and praline. Candied lemon peel may be substituted if citron is not available. For variation, dried currants may be substituted for the candied fruit, and white sugar may replace the brown.

Half of the squares are coated with milk chocolate and the other half with dark chocolate. To achieve their marbled effect, spread the melted milk chocolate thinly on a mottled-texture plexiglass board and the melted dark chocolate on a differently-textured plexiglass surface. Then the ganache squares which have been dipped in dark chocolate are gently placed on the milk chocolate board, and the squares dipped in milk chocolate

on the dark chocolate board. After allowing them to cool for about 20 minutes, each square can be lifted off the plexiglass with a little twist. The finished surface of the squares should appear shiny and firm, marbled with different colors and textures of chocolate to please the eye as well as the palate.

The praline ganache may be kept overnight at 62.6 °F/17 °C before being napped with the tempered chocolate. The finished marbled squares can be covered with plastic wrap and kept for about one month at room temperature (62.6 °F/17 °C) on their original plastic board. To preserve their shape and texture, do not lift them off the board until you wish to serve them.

Gourmets and chocolate-lovers, beware: These Marbled Squares are simply impossible to resist!

1. To make hazelnut praline, combine the nuts and sugar in a heavy-bottomed pot and cook for a few minutes until the insides of the nuts turn a rich amber color (check by splitting one open). Pour the praline onto an oiled plate or baking sheet, let cool, then grind in a blender or food processor until it is the texture of coarse sand.

2. For the ganache, melt the milk chocolate in a double boiler until it reaches 84.2 °F/29 °C. Mix the praline into the melted chocolate. Cover a baking sheet with plastic wrap, place a square frame on top, and pour the ganache mixture into the frame. Sprinkle the chopped candied citrus fruits onto the square.

Squares

3. Smooth the surface with a spatula and set aside at room temperature (64.4–68 °F/18–20 °C). When the block has set, carefully unmold the frame, sliding a knife along the edges if necessary. Cut into small squares, heating the knife blade between cuts.

4. To finish, melt the tempered milk chocolate (to 84.2 °F/29 °C) and dark chocolate (to 87.8 °F/31 °C) in separate double boilers. Using a fork, dip half the squares in the milk chocolate, and the other half in the dark chocolate. Place on a plastic board to cool, then marble the chocolates as described in the text above.

Creole Delights

For the base layer:
⅔ cup/150 g butter
1 cup/250 g sugar
scant ⅓ cup/100 g honey
⅔ cup/150 ml heavy cream
6½ tbsp/100 ml glucose syrup
1⅓ cups/250 g candied orange peel
⅔ cup/100 g dried papaya
¾ cup plus 1 tbsp/100 g flour
generous 2 cups/250 g slivered almonds

For the almond brittle or "nougatine" (optional):
1¼ cups/300 g sugar
¾ cup/200 ml glucose syrup
generous 2 cups/250 g slivered almonds or 2 cups/300 g chopped almonds

For the coating:
7 oz/200 g tempered dark chocolate
7 oz/200 g tempered white chocolate
7 oz/200 g tempered milk chocolate

Makes: 40 chocolates
Preparation time: 30 minutes
Cooking time: 6 minutes
Difficulty: ★

These Creole Delights, or "Créolines," were inspired by the famous recipe for florentines: Suave chocolate circles sit atop a creamy, chewy confection of cookie, caramel, nuts and fruit, all smothered in rich chocolate. Yum!

The creolines may of course be served on an elegant tray, but if time permits, making a nougatine "dish" will give an unforgettable dramatic finish. The almond brittle, or nougatine, is made by gently heating the glucose over moderate heat, without allowing it to boil. Then the sugar is added and cooked until it turns a light caramel color. Next the almonds are stirred in, and finally the mixture is poured onto a sheet of plastic wrap,

covered with another sheet of plastic wrap, and carefully rolled out with a rolling pin.

While the mixture is still hot, the edge of the nougatine can be decoratively cut or fluted. Press the nougatine onto an upturned serving dish to create a bowl shape. When cool, the nougatine "dish" is filled with the Créolines for a stunning—and completely edible!—presentation.

These petits fours are coated in three different colors of chocolate for an attractive look, but if time is short, just one or two kinds of chocolate may be used, making sure that the total quantity is the same.

1. For the créoline bases, melt the butter and sugar in a pot. Add the honey, cream and glucose syrup.

2. Cook the mixture until it reaches 246 °F/119 °C. Remove from heat and add the finely chopped orange peel and papaya, the flour and the slivered almonds. Mix well. Make the nougatine according to the directions in the text above.

("Créolines")

3. Roll the créoline mixture into long logs about 1 in/2.5 cm in diameter, then slice rounds about ⅜ in/1 cm thick. Butter and flour a muffin pan, or line with paper cupcake cups. Place each "cookie" in a cup and bake at 355 °F/180 °C for 6 minutes. Cool.

4. Melt each type of tempered chocolate separately. Pour a thin layer into circular patterned molds, and press a créoline "cookie" gently into each melted chocolate circle. Cool at least 1 hour at room temperature. Unmold and serve.

Elegant

20 cherries, marinated in rum
7 oz/200 g fondant (see
    basic recipe)
1 tsp/5 g freshly ground white pepper
3½ tbsp/50 g dark rum

To finish:
12 oz/350 g tempered dark chocolate

Makes:	20 chocolate-covered cherries
Preparation time:	40 minutes
Difficulty:	★

With their refined appearance and baroque taste, these divine chocolate-covered cherries recall the aristocratic Frenchwomen of the 17th century. Whole cherries marinated in rum or other liqueurs may be purchsed at gourmet shops, but are also easy to make at home. Choose ripe, firm, unblemished fruits with the stems attached. Place them in a sterilized quart jar and cover with good rum. A cinnamon stick and a clove or two may be added for extra flavor before leaving the cherries to macerate for several months.

Fondant is a simply and versatile kind of sweet creamy icing which may be purchased from specialist candy suppliers, or simply made at home (see basic recipe).

Once the cherries have been coated in chocolate, they should again be left for several days before serving, to allow the fondant time to absorb the flavors of cherry and rum. The chocolate blanket serves to keep the cherries soaked in liqueur until the moment they are eaten.

When making chocolate "leaves," painting the upper side of the real leaves will result in shiny chocolate "leaves" but without the distinctive leaf pattern. If the coating is painted on the underside, the chocolate "leaf" will have a duller surface but a realistic veined look and texture.

1. Remove the steeped cherries from the jar of rum and drain on paper towel.

2. Melt the fondant in a double boiler, add the ground pepper and rum, and blend well. Dip the cherries in the hot fondant,then place on a sheet of wax paper to cool and harden, about 10 minutes.

Island Cherries

3. Melt the dark chocolate in a double boiler until it reaches 87.8 °F/31 °C. Dip the fondant-covered cherries in the melted chocolate, covering them completely until the chocolate covers ⅜ in/1 cm of the stem. Place on a sheet of wax paper and set aside in a cool place.

4. Make the chocolate "leaves" by painting the surface of real leaves with a pastry brush dipped in melted tempered dark chocolate. Let them cool for about 30 minutes before carefully peeling off the real leaves. Serve the cherries on an elegant dish garnished with chocolate leaves.

Tangy

For the ganache:
2 tbsp/30 ml passion fruit juice
1½ tbsp/20 ml papaya juice
1½ tbsp/20 ml pineapple juice
1½ tbsp/20 ml orange juice
5¼ oz/150 g white chocolate
¾ oz/20 g milk chocolate
2 tbsp/30 g cocoa butter
1½ tbsp/20 g butter
6½ tbsp/100 ml dark rum

To finish:
5¼ oz/150 g tempered white chocolate
1 tbsp/10 g tempered dark chocolate
3 oz/90 g tempered milk chocolate

Makes:	30 squares
Preparation time:	40 minutes
Difficulty:	★ ★

This delectable ganache is created with a unique cocktail of fruit juices. The variety of juices may be modified so long as it includes a balance of sweet and tangy flavors, and the same total quantity of liquid. The rum, may also be replaced with another liqueur, such as Grand Marnier.

Most often a ganache contains cream, but because this ganache contains so much juice, it requires both butter and cocoa butter to help it thicken to the right consistency.

The decorative coating on these squares is easy to make. Once the squares have been dipped in the white chocolate, fill a wax paper cone or pastry bag with dark chocolate, melted to 87.8 °F/31 °C. The tip of the cone is then gently pressed into the white chocolate surface while squeezing the dark chocolate onto the squares, thus mixing the two colors in a marbled pattern. Small pieces of heavy-duty plastic wrap just larger than the white squares are then placed on each candy and pressed, gently and evenly, onto the surface.

These tangy squares are full of vitamins, and are perfect served with a cup of tea for a refreshing "pick-me-up" toward the end of a long day.

1. Combine the fruit juices in a pot and heat on high heat. Chop the white and milk chocolate for the ganache and place in a mixing bowl. Pour the boiling juices onto the chocolate and blend. Melt the cocoa butter and add to the mixture, then add the cold butter and stir. Mix in the rum and set aside.

2. When the ganache has cooled to the consistency of soft butter, cover a board or baking sheet with plastic wrap, place a square frame on top, and pour the ganache into the frame.

Squares

3. Smooth the surface of the ganache with a spatula and set aside at room temperature (62.6–68 °F/17–20 °C) to cool and harden, about 15–20 minutes. Then remove the frame. Melt the tempered milk chocolate in a double boiler until it reaches 84.2 °F/29 °C. Frost the ganache block with the melted milk chocolate and smooth the surface with a spatula.

4. Cut the block into small squares when firm. To finish, melt the tempered white chocolate to 82.4 °F/28 °C. Dip each square into the melted chocolate, then place on a sheet of wax paper to cool. Melt the dark chocolate and fill a paper cone or pastry bag. Decorate each square for a marbled effect, then cover each one with a piece of plastic wrap, pressing evenly. Cool until firm.

For the ganache:
5 tbsp/75 ml pineapple juice
    or 1 ripe whole pineapple
3½ oz/100 g white chocolate
1 oz/30 g dark chocolate
3 tbsp/45 ml heavy cream
2 tbsp/30 ml lychee liqueur
scant ½ cup/50 g cocoa butter, melted

For the base layers:
1¾ oz/50 g tempered dark chocolate

Makes: 40–50 chocolates
Preparation time: 30 minutes
Difficulty: ★

Pineapple is the ultimate taste of the islands: juicy, refreshing, tangy, delicious!

Fresh whole pineapples should be truly ripe and fragrant to be at their juiciest. For variety, fresh lychees or cherimoyas could be substituted. Another type of liqueur could be substituted for lychee, provided it blends well with the fruit. Alcohol is generally a useful addition to ganache, not only for the flavor it adds, but also because it helps to preserve the chocolates!

Chocolate, like mayonnaise, is an emulsion, and must be handled with care to prevent the fat from separating out.

Separation may also occur due to inferior quality chocolate or simply too high a fat content. And just as curdled mayonnaise may be restored by beating in a few drops of vinegar, if the ganache seems to turn lumpy or grainy during cooking, it can be rectified by adding a few teaspoons more alcohol while stirring briskly with a whisk.

In this recipe, dark chocolate bases are covered artistically with luscious fruity ganache. The decorative "kiss" shapes are meant to imitate pineapple skin, but any creative design will please the eye as well as the taste buds.

1. Peel the fresh pineapple, cut it into chunks, purée in a blender or food processor and strain, retaining the juice. Chop the white and dark chocolate and place in a round-bottomed mixing bowl.

2. Combine the pineapple juice and cream in a pot and bring to a boil. Remove from the heat, add the lychee liqueur and the melted cocoa butter, and blend. Pour the hot mixture over the chopped chocolate and stir.

Kisses

3. Knead the ganache with a rubber or plastic spatula or scraper until it is smooth. To make the base layers, melt the dark chocolate in a double boiler until it reaches 87.8 °F/31 °C. Dip a fingertip in the melted chocolate and dab 40–50 oval shapes on a sheet of wax paper. Set these bases aside to cool.

4. Fill a pastry bag with the cooled ganache and, using a small nozzle, squeeze a series of "kisses" onto each oval base. Then fill a paper cone or pastry bag with any remaining dark chocolate to decorate the kisses. Set the chocolates aside at room temperature (62.6–68 °F/17–20 °C) to cool and harden.

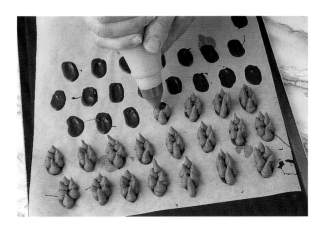

Passion Fruit

For the ganache:
6½ tbsp/100 ml passion fruit juice
6½ tbsp/100 ml heavy cream
1½ tbsp/20 g butter
the grated rind of half a lime
5½ oz/160 g milk chocolate
3½ oz/100 g dark chocolate

To finish:
8¾ oz/250 g tempered dark chocolate
unsweetened cocoa powder
confectioners' sugar

Makes:	40 truffles
Preparation time:	25 minutes
Difficulty:	★

If pepper is the professional confectioner's salt, limes are known as the "chocolate-maker's pepper"! Finely grated lime rind heightens the flavor of these rich but refreshing treats, while the ganache derives its silken smoothness from an extra portion of butter. Other tart fruits may be substituted for the passion fruit, for instance, lemon, lime or grapefruit; but the right acid balance is very important. Oranges, for example, are not tangy enough for this recipe.

These truffles are coated with dark chocolate, though milk chocolate may be used instead, provided that the maximum reheating temperature of 84.2 °F/29 °C is respected.

The truffles may be served piled into a pyramid and dusted with unsweetened cocoa powder or confectioners' sugar. Another way to garnish is to fill a wax paper cone with melted chocolate and squeeze long parallel lines across the serving dish before arranging the truffles on it.

1. For the ganache, combine the passion fruit juice, cream, butter and finely grated lime rind in a pot. Bring to a boil.

2. Chop the milk and dark chocolate. Remove the boiling mixture from the heat and add the chopped chocolate, stir, and set aside to cool until it reaches 59–62.6 °F/15–17 °C.

Truffles

3. To finish, melt the tempered dark chocolate in a double boiler until it reaches 87.8 °F/31 °C.

4. Fill a pastry bag with the ganache and squeeze balls onto a sheet of wax paper. Set aside at room temperature (62.6 °F/17 °C) for 30 minutes. When the ganache balls are firm, dip them in the melted chocolate, then dust with unsweetened cocoa powder. Dust the serving dish with confectioners' sugar.

Cinnamon

For the ganache:
⅔ cup/150 ml heavy cream
1 cinnamon stick
1 tsp/5 g ground cinnamon
6 oz/170 g milk chocolate

To finish:
5¼ oz/150 g tempered dark chocolate
⅓ cup/70 g cinnamon powder

Makes:	40 truffles
Preparation time:	20 minutes
Difficulty:	★

These delectable, spicy, melt-in-your mouth truffles make wonderful holiday gifts.

The warm glow of the cinnamon is intensified if a spoonful of orange-flavored liqueur or other spirit is added to the ganache. In this case, to keep the correct proportions of liquid, subtract an equivalent amount of cream.

To create other variations, tempered white or milk chocolate may be substituted for the dark chocolate coating. Those who prefer a less intense cinnamon flavor may use unsweetened cocoa powder or confectioners' sugar to dust the truffles. Rolling the coated chocolate logs in finely chopped, roasted almonds is another way to lend an extra dash of finesse.

If time permits, a marbled chocolate "serving dish" may be created by melting different chocolates according to the directions for tempering (see p. 52). Spread them on a sheet of heavy-duty plastic wrap, mix partially for a marbled effect, then shape the melted chocolate into a free-form dish and let it cool at 62.6 °F/17 °C for at least half an hour. Then carefully peel off the plastic and arrange the truffles elegantly on their customized chocolate dish.

1. For the ganache, boil the cream in a pot with the cinnamon stick and ground cinnamon.

2. Chop the milk chocolate, place in a mixing bowl, and pour the boiling cream over it. Stir and set aside to cool.

Truffles

3. Fill a pastry bag with the ganache and squeeze short thick logs (about 1¼ in/3 cm long) onto a sheet of wax paper. Set aside in a cool place for 15 minutes. Melt the tempered dark chocolate in a double boiler until it reaches 87.8 °F/31 °C. Using a fork, dip each ganache log into the melted dark chocolate to coat.

4. Immediately dip each coated log in the cinnamon powder, rolling it with a fork until completely covered with cinnamon. Imprint with the fork tines for decoration, then arrange on a serving dish.

Carnival

For the nougat:
2 large egg whites
scant ¼ cup/75 g honey
6½ tbsp/100 g white sugar
2 tbsp/30 g cocoa butter, melted
2½ tbsp/40 ml papaya juice
⅔ cup/75 g slivered almonds
¼ cup/30 g bright green pistachios
¼ cup/50 g candied fruit
⅛ cup/25 g dark raisins

To finish:
¾ oz/20 g tempered dark chocolate

Makes: 40–50 pieces
Preparation time: 30 minutes
Cooking time: 17 minutes
Difficulty: ★ ★

Nougat never goes out of style. It is famous for its sweet, chewy texture, which seems somehow to fulfill our secret desires. With its festive carnival-colored fruits and crunchy nuts, this nougat is worthy of Mardi Gras itself.

Traditional nougat has been adapted for this recipe with great style, but one tricky step should be noted: Great care must be taken when mixing the honey and sugar into the egg whites. First, set the electric mixer on maximum speed while adding the heated honey (244.4 °F/118 °C) in a ribbon to the beaten egg whites. Then, immediately add the hot cooked sugar (305.6 °F/ 152 °C) in a ribbon, beating constantly the whole time. These two steps are absolutely essential to making successful nougat. If these steps are not performed quickly, the sugar and egg whites may mix unevenly, creating lumps of cooked egg and crystallized sugar that are impossible to salvage.

Here is a professional chef's trick for beating high foamy egg whites: Add a pinch of sugar to prevent the whites from separating or becoming "grainy."

The flavor of the nougat may be varied by using different types of honey, or by substituting pineapple, mango, cherimoya or passion fruit juice for the papaya juice.

1. Beat the egg whites and a pinch of sugar with an electric mixer until foamy. Heat the honey in a pot until it reaches 244.4 °F/118 °C, about 6–7 minutes, then pour in a thin ribbon onto the egg whites while continuing to beat on high speed.

2. Meanwhile, cook the sugar separately on high heat for about 10 minutes, until it reaches 305.6 °F/152 °C. Check the temperature on a candy thermometer. Then pour the cooked sugar in a thin ribbon onto the honey-egg white mixture, still beating on high speed. Finally, add the melted cocoa butter, and stop beating.

Nougat

3. Dice the candied fruit into small pieces and chop the pistachios finely. Add the fruit, pistachios, and raisins to the nougat mixture, stirring with a wooden spatula. Melt the tempered dark chocolate in a double boiler until it reaches 87.8 °F/31 °C.

4. Pour the hot nougat mixture onto a sheet of plastic wrap, cover it with more plastic wrap, then roll to an even thickness with a rolling pin. Let cool for 30 minutes at room temperature. Cut the nougat into small squares. Dip some of the squares in the melted dark chocolate and cool until firm.

Banana-Papaya and

For the banana-papaya jelly squares:
½ lb/250 g papaya flesh
2 tsp/8 g pectin
2 tbsp/30 g superfine sugar
1¼ cups/300 g coarse sugar
½ cup/125 ml glucose syrup
½ lb/250 g bananas
4 tsp/20 ml lime juice
2 tsp/8 g citric acid solution (1 tsp/4 g citric
   acid + 1 tsp/4 ml boiling water)

For the kiwi-kumquat jelly squares:
1 cup/250 g kiwi flesh
¾ cup/200 ml kumquat juice
2 tbsp/30 g superfine sugar
2 tsp/8 g pectin
1¼ cups/300 g coarse sugar
½ cup/125 g glucose syrup
1½ tbsp/20 ml lime juice
2 tsp/8 g citric acid solution (1 tsp/4 g citric
   acid + 1 tsp/4 g boiling water)

To finish:
¼ cup/50 g superfine sugar

Serves	6
Preparation time:	25 minutes
Resting time:	1 hour
Cooking time:	15 minutes
Difficulty:	★ ★

Success with these fruit jelly squares requires a little patience, some dexterity, and above all speed. A candy thermometer is also essential to precisely monitor the stages of cooking.

For the kiwi-kumquat jelly squares, the following procedure is recommended: First, the kiwi pulp is heated to 104 °F/40 °C. In another dish, the pectin and superfine sugar are mixed, then sprinkled over the cooked kiwi, which is kept at 104 °F/40 °C. The mixture is then whisked briskly and brought to a boil for one minute. Continue stirring while adding the coarse sugar and glucose bit by bit, and cook the mixture just until it reaches

228 °F/109 °C. This temperature must be maintained while gradually adding the kumquat and lime juices. The moment the mixture reaches 230 °F/110 °C, it should be removed from the heat and the citric acid solution added. Then the fruit jelly must be poured immediately into a cake pan lined with plastic wrap.

Citric acid powder is essential for making jellied fruit squares. It can be found at pharmacies or specialist candy supply merchants. Mixed with boiling water, it makes a solution that helps to balance the flavors and set the fruit mixture.

1. Heat the papaya in a pot. Add the pectin and superfine sugar, mix well, then bring to a boil for one minute. Add the coarse sugar little by little, then the glucose, and heat to 228 °F/109 °C.

2. Mash the bananas with a fork, then stir in the lime juice. Keep the papaya boiling and slowly add the mashed banana-lime juice, maintaining the mixture at 228 °F/109 °C. As soon as the mixture reaches 230 °F/110 °C, remove from the heat and add the citric acid solution.

Kiwi-Kumquat Jelly Squares

3. Immediately pour the mixture into a cake pan lined with plastic wrap, and let sit for 1 hour. Follow the same procedure to make the kiwi-kumquat jelly squares.

4. Unmold the jelly and cut into small squares. To finish, roll the squares in superfine sugar, and arrange creatively on a serving dish.

Rose

For the ganache:
6½ tbsp/100 ml heavy cream
12-15 red rose petals
2 tsp/10 ml orange-flower water
5¼ oz/150 g white chocolate

For the decoration:
4½ tbsp/70 ml water
generous ½ cup/150 g superfine sugar
2 perfectly blossomed red roses
3½ oz/100 g tempered dark chocolate

Serves   4
Preparation time: 25 minutes
Difficulty: ★

Roses, the queen of flowers, symbolize magic, love and romance. A verse written by the French poet Ronsard is perfect to dedicate this inspired floral confection: "Let us observe the dainty rose, who just this morning to blossom chose, with dew-drop pearls upon its petals..."

In this stunning recipe, dainty ganache rose pearls are presented on a bed of dark chocolate and candied leaves. The rather unusual combination of white chocolate and orange-flower water tastes almost like roses, and the preparation of the ganache is so simple that more time can be spent on the elaborate presentation.

To make the dark chocolate bases, cut squares of wax paper measuring 4 x 1¼ in/10 x 3 cm. Melt dark chocolate (heated to 87.8 °F/31 °C, or milk chocolate to 84.2 °F/29 °C) and spread it to an even thickness on each square. When the bases are barely firm, mold them to the desired shape, remove the wax paper, and position on the serving dish.

Rose leaves may be candied in sugar syrup (see basic recipe) or may be coated in chocolate, but care must be taken as the leaves are rather fragile. Make sure that the rose leaves as well as blossoms are free from any type of pesticide.

1. Put the cream in a pot and float the 12–15 rose petals in the cream, then bring to a boil.

2. Add the orange-flower water, then put the mixture through a blender or food processor, petals and all. Chop the white chocolate and place in a mixing bowl, then pour the hot, puréed cream mixture onto the chocolate. Stir and set aside.

Pearls

3. Make a sugar syrup by boiling the water and the sugar until it reaches 98.6 °F/37° C. Then crystallize each petal of the blossomed roses by dipping one finger into the sugar syrup and coating the inside of each petal with your finger. Immediately sprinkle this syrup-coated side with sugar so that it sticks to the petal.

4. Arrange the dark chocolate bases on a serving dish and lay the sugared petals on top. Fill a pastry bag with the ganache, and squeeze a dollop onto the base of each rose petal. Garnish the plate with rose leaves, chill for 1 hour and serve.

Diamonds in

For the ganache:
3½ oz/100 g dark chocolate
2½ oz/70 g milk chocolate
6½ tbsp/100 ml heavy cream
1 vanilla bean
a pinch of pink and black pepper
6½ tbsp/100 ml banana liqueur

To finish:
7 oz/200 g tempered milk chocolate

Makes: 30 chocolates
Preparation time: 30 minutes
Difficulty: ★

Chocolate is the perfect antidote to the stressful modern lifestyle: It is truly a source of energy and good health, filled with vitamins and minerals, and a taste that can brighten the most difficult day. The Aztecs considered chocolate an aphrodisiac and allowed only the Emperor and his court to drink it. Perhaps they were right; modern scientists have found that chocolate contains phenylethylamine and other substances that produce a natural euphoria!

The pink and black pepper add punch to this ganache, while the banana liqueur gives it a rich, exotic savor. The ganache may be artfully cut into squares, diamonds, or rectangles, using a sharp knife with its blade heated in a flame or in hot water to make clean, crisp edges. If the knife is dipped in water, it is important to carefully wipe the blade clean and dry before making each cut.

Dark, white, or colored chocolate may be substituted for the milk chocolate finishing coat, but in each case the squares should be cooled on differently textured plexiglass boards to create the "diamond" effect.

These luscious diamond-faceted chocolates will add an elegant sparkle to your dinner parties!

1. Chop the milk and dark chocolate for the ganache and place in a mixing bowl. Boil the cream with the scraped-out pulp of the vanilla bean and the ground pepper, then pour over the chocolate and stir.

2. Gently whisk in the banana liqueur. Set aside at room temperature (62.6–68 °F/17–20 °C) for 15 minutes. Then pour the ganache into a frame placed on a board covered with plastic wrap, smooth the surface, and let harden for 10 minutes at room temperature.

the Rough

3. Melt the tempered milk chocolate in a double boiler until it reaches 84.2 °F/29 °C. Unmold the block of ganache and cover it with some of the melted milk chocolate. Let it cool until firm. Cut into squares with a sharp knife, cleaning and heating the blade in flame between each cut.

4. Using a fork, dip each square into the milk chocolate and place on a textured plexiglass board. Allow the squares to cool until firm, then remove by giving the board a slight twist. Enjoy!

Chocolate-Covered

For the chocolates:
5¼ oz/150 g fondant (see basic
    recipe)
12 surettes, steeped in spiced rum
10½ oz/300 g tempered dark chocolate

For the decoration:
3½ tbsp/50 g green marzipan
3½ tbsp/50 g pink or white marzipan

Serves	*4*
Preparation time:	*20 minutes*
Cooking time:	*10 minutes*
Chilling time:	*10 minutes*
Difficulty:	*★*

These obsidian fruits are hardly known in the USA, yet there are over 400 species growing in the tropics! The variety used here is grown in Martinique, and is called *surette* or "sour fruit." It is usually eaten fresh or as compote.

This recipe calls for surettes that have been steeped in rum spiked with cinnamon and vanilla for several months (see the instructions given for cherries on p. 102). If surettes are unavailable, try using small dark plums instead. The alcohol-soaked fruit should be carefully drained on paper towel before being dipped in fondant and then coated with chocolate.

Great care should be taken to leave the stems attached throughout the process, both to facilitate dipping and to give the fruit an attractive, natural look.

The fondant may be store-bought, but is usually better homemade (see basic recipe). Fondant is made of sugar and glucose which are cooked to a syrup. It is then kneaded with a spatula until it thickens, then kneaded again by hand until it is a perfectly smooth, stiff white paste. Fondant may be made ahead of time, as it keeps perfectly in an airtight container.

Fondant can be used plain or flavored, for example, with chocolate, coffee, strawberry, lemon or orange. In pastry it is often used to nap the surface of cakes such as génoise, millefeuilles or eclairs.

These singularly elegant fruit treats are sure to be a hit with your lucky guests!

1. Place a round-bottomed mixing bowl over a pan of simmering water, like a double boiler, and melt the fondant for about 5 minutes while stirring.

2. Cover ¾ of each fruit with fondant by holding the stem and dipping as pictured. Remove any excess fondant with a spoon. Lay the fruit on a sheet of wax paper to harden for 10 minutes.

Surettes

3. Melt the dark chocolate in another round-bottomed mixing bowl over a pan of simmering water, like a double boiler, for about 5 minutes, stirring constantly. Dip the fondant-covered fruit completely in the chocolate, remove any excess with a spoon, and lay the fruit on a tray. Refrigerate immediately.

4. With a rolling pin, evenly roll the green marzipan as shown, then dust the surface with confectioners' sugar. Cut out 36 leaf shapes and draw the veins in the leaves with a knife tip. Wrap each chocolate-covered surette with 3 marzipan leaves. Roll out the pink or white marzipan and make a rose for decoration.

For the ganache:
6½ tbsp/100 g superfine sugar
⅓ cup/80 ml heavy cream, lightly whipped
1½ tbsp/20 g very finely ground coffee
4½ oz/130 g milk chocolate
5 tsp/25 g butter
¾ cup/200 ml Shrubb or other orange-
    flavored liqueur

To finish:
7 oz/200 g tempered dark chocolate
¼ cup/50 g very finely ground espresso
    coffee

Makes: 40 truffles
Preparation time: 35 minutes
Cooking time: a few minutes
Difficulty: ★

Chocoholics and coffee fans alike will love these incredible truffles. They are quite simple to make, and have the virtue of being protein-filled, as well as therapeutic and stress-relieving. Their heavenly taste derives in part from Shrubb, a delicious tropical liqueur made of orange rind steeped in rum. Other types of rum or orange-flavored liqueur may also be used with great success, for example, dark aged rum, white rum, or mandarine-flavored Napoleon.

As always, safety precautions are important when working with cooked sugar. It is imperative that the cream be lightly whipped before adding it to the caramel, because if liquid cream is added it could boil up and overflow. Partially whipping the cream beforehand incorporates air, which allows it to blend with the cooked sugar without "spitting," thus reducing the risk of burning yourself.

The ganache should be blended thoroughly until it is smooth to eliminate any air bubbles before it is put into a pastry bag.

These truffles are presented in the shape of balls, but may also be made into logs, which are easier to roll in the ground espresso. The espresso coffee should be of a strong, well-flavored variety such as Kenyan, and must be ground as finely as possible to release the richest taste. For variety, the truffles may also be rolled in unsweetened cocoa powder, or confectioners' sugar flavored with vanilla or spices.

1. Cook the sugar in a heavy-bottomed pan for a few minutes until it turns to caramel. Immediately remove from the heat and whisk in the whipped cream. Add the ground coffee and bring to a boil. Chop the milk chocolate for the ganache and place in a mixing bowl with the butter. Pour the boiling mixture over the chocolate and butter, and stir. Add the orange-flavored liqueur and mix well.

2. Let the ganache cool for about 15 minutes at 62.6 °F/17 °C. Stir again until smooth. Fill a pastry bag with ganache and squeeze balls onto a sheet of wax paper. Set aside to cool for 15 minutes.

Shrubb Truffles

3. For a nice round shape, roll each ball in your palms, dusted with unsweetened cocoa powder to avoid sticking.

4. To finish, melt the tempered dark chocolate in a double boiler until it reaches 87.8 °F/31 °C. Dip each ball in the chocolate using a fork, then roll in the ground espresso.

Amber Rum

For the ganache:
8¾ oz/250 g dark chocolate
⅔ cup/150 ml heavy cream
1¼ cups/300 ml dark rum
2 tbsp crème fraîche
1 tbsp glucose syrup

For the coating:
4½ cups/500 g unsweetened cocoa powder

Serves	4
Preparation time:	45 minutes
Cooking time:	7-8 minutes
Chilling time:	1 hour
Difficulty:	★

Real truffles are in fact small, round, black mushrooms, also known as "black diamonds," usually found buried in the ground around oak trees. The writer George Sand poetically called them "fairy potatoes." Like their namesakes, these delicious truffles are a rare and precious delicacy, but with the fine taste of chocolate.

In France, chocolate truffles are considered so extravagant that they are usually reserved for holidays or special occasions.

For this recipe, the chocolate may be melted either in a double boiler or over direct heat, but it must be heated slowly so it retains its taste and shine. It should first be chopped, then melted and stirred gently with a spatula for a smooth, creamy texture. Here the ganache is flavored with rum, but brandy, whisky, vanilla or lychee liqueur will also do nicely.

Crème fraîche has a texture similar to, but a less sour taste than, American sour cream and can be cooked at higher heat without separating, and is thus an essential ingredient in many French sauces, for example. It may be found at fine grocers, or simply made at home (see recipe in glossary).

These truffles may be kept longer if they are refrigerated, and can even be frozen. They go wonderfully well with tea or coffee. Wrapped in an elegant box or package, they make a personal and always much-appreciated gift.

1. For the ganache, slowly melt the chopped chocolate in a double boiler, stirring constantly. When melted, add the heavy cream, glucose and rum. Stir briskly, then blend in the crème fraîche. Cook for 7–8 minutes, then cover with plastic wrap and refrigerate for 30 minutes.

2. Dip a melon baller or spoon in hot water and wipe it dry, then scoop out balls of ganache. Place on a tray or sheet of wax paper.

Truffles

3. For an even round shape, dip the balls in unsweetened cocoa powder, then roll between your palms.

4. Roll the balls again in the unsweetened cocoa powder. Refrigerate for 30 minutes before serving on an elegant plate.

Breads
and
Pastries

Lime Passion

10 tbsp/150 g butter, softened
1⅔ cups/250 g confectioners' sugar
finely grated rind of 1 lime
6 egg whites
1⅔ cups/200 g flour, sifted

To finish:
5¼ oz/150 g fondant
½ cup/100 g passion fruit flesh
1¾ oz/50 g dark chocolate
a few drops food coloring

Makes:	50 cookies
Preparation time:	30 minutes
Baking time:	15 minutes
Difficulty:	★

These delicate, crunchy cookies can last a long time, but are usually devoured quickly! They are especially delicious served with lime or passion fruit sherbet, and also complement vanilla or chocolate ice cream, fruit or chocolate mousse. Passion fruit was chosen for this recipe, but any other exotic fruit—pineapples, cherimoya, or mango—will substitute nicely.

Making the cookie dough is quite easy, but it must be closely monitored when baking, as the cookies burn easily.

The fondant should be warmed up to body temperature (98.6 °F/37 °C) before use. This can be measured with a candy thermometer, or simply with a finger dipped in fondant and touched to the lower lip; the fondant should feel neither warm nor cool to the touch. To decorate the cookies, frost with the fondant, then cool, then paint the frosted surface with melted dark chocolate for a marbled effect.

For a festive, colorful decoration, stripes of food coloring can be added immediately after the chocolate. Just let a few drops slide down the tip of a knife and indent the stripes by pulling the knife tip very gently through the fondant.

1. Preheat the oven to 375 °F/190 °C. Beat the butter and sugar in a large mixing bowl with an electric mixer until the mixture is smooth and creamy. Add the grated lime rind.

2. Beat in the egg whites little by little on slow speed, then gradually add the sifted flour.

Fruit Cookies

3. Grease the baking sheets or line them with parchment paper. Put the cookie dough in a pastry bag and squeeze "logs" onto the baking sheets. Bake for 15 minutes at 375 °F/190 °C. As soon as the cookies come out of the oven, remove them to cooling racks with a spatula.

4. Heat the fondant to 98.6 °F/37 °C. Blend in the passion fruit, then dip each cooled cookie into the fondant. Melt the dark chocolate in a double boiler, fill a paper cone or pastry bag with it, and draw a marbled pattern on the cookies.

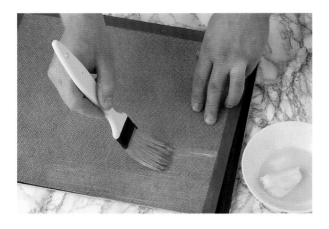

Mini-Brioche

For the dough:
3½ tbsp/50 ml water
4 cups/500 g white flour, sifted
2 tsp/10 g salt
¼ cup/60 g sugar
3 eggs
¾ oz/20 g yeast
10 tbsp/150 g butter

To finish:
1 egg, slightly beaten
3½ tbsp/50 g granulated cane sugar

Makes:	*20 small brioche*
Preparation time:	*20 minutes*
Chilling and rising time:	*1 hour 15 minutes*
Baking time:	*30 minutes*
Difficulty:	★

The origin of the word brioche is controversial, but one thing is certain: These buttery, light pastries are deliciously satisfying, eaten for breakfast or with afternoon tea, as an after-school or after-work snack. A cross between bread and cake, brioche are easy to make, and with a sprinkling of cane sugar on top, are a sweet reminder of the islands.

To make brioche light and well-risen, the proportions of butter, eggs and water must be carefully maintained, though the water may be replaced with milk for a richer taste. Ideally, the dough should be made ahead of time and left to rise overnight in the refrigerator. The secret to success with brioche dough is to mix thoroughly before the butter is added to develop a fine

texture. The butter must be cool, soft but not oily, when it is beaten in bit by bit. The dough may break up when the butter is first added, but will gradually come together again.

Brioche dough may be also braided or shaped into a wreath, and garnished with dark or golden raisins. For those who seek a stronger island flavor, a few teaspoons of rum may be added to the egg glaze for the surface.

The oven should be preheated for at least 10 minutes at a higher heat, then reduced to the correct baking temperature of 355 °F/180 °C when the brioche go into the oven.

Filling these mini-brioche with kiwano, mango or guava jam is an excellent way to add an exotic note.

1. In a large mixing bowl, combine the water, flour, salt, and sugar. Add the eggs one by one, blending well. Then add the yeast and softened butter. Keep beating until the dough makes a ball that no longer sticks to the sides of the bowl.

2. Turn the dough onto a clean dry cloth, wrap and refrigerate about 15 minutes.

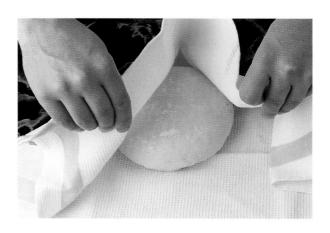

with Cane Sugar

3. Divide the dough into pieces weighing about 1½ oz/40 g each, and shape into balls or logs. Set aside on a covered baking dish to rise until doubled in size, about 1 hour.

4. Paint the surface of each brioche with a pastry brush dipped in the beaten egg. Use scissors or a knife to slash a cross-shaped decorative incision on the surface of each brioche. Sprinkle with granulated cane sugar, and bake 30 minutes at 355 °F/180 °C.

Banana

For the puff pastry:
  (see basic recipe)
4 cups/500 g flour
1⅔ cups/400 g butter
2 tsp/10 g salt
1¼ cups/300 ml water

For the filling:
2 very ripe bananas
2 tsp/10 g butter
3½ tbsp/50 ml aged dark rum
4 tsp/20 g white sugar
1 egg, slightly beaten

Makes: 25 turnovers
Preparation time: 30 minutes
Baking time: 20 minutes
Difficulty: ★

Bananas and rum are a classic combination, here innovatively combined in an original pastry recipe. The bananas should be very ripe so they are easy to mash and blend with the rum. Or flambée the bananas in the rum at the end of cooking, for an even more intense taste. Other liquids may be used, for instance banana or coconut liqueur, or simply fruit juice for those who do not wish to use alcohol.

Brushing the turnovers with lightly beaten egg before baking gives the pastry surface a wonderfully appetizing, shiny golden amber color. A pinch of salt may be added to the egg to make it more liquid and easier to paint on.

Puff pastry is not difficult to make, but time can be saved by buying it ready-made, or by making it ahead of time and storing it in the freezer in a sealed plastic bag or container.

When the turnovers have finished baking, they should be placed on a cake rack to cool, as this will help the steam evaporate away from the pastry.

These turnovers should be served freshly made, hot or warm, dusted with confectioners' sugar. If they were made the day before, they can be reheated in a moderate oven (not a microwave as this turns the pastry soggy!) and served for breakfast with fresh hot coffee and a glass of fruit juice.

1. Make the puff pastry (see basic recipe). Roll it out evenly and cut out circles. Roll each circle to an oval shape, place on a non-stick baking sheet, and set aside.

2. In a pot, slowly melt the butter and slice the peeled bananas into it.

Rum Turnovers

3. Add the sugar and rum and cook over high heat about 5 minutes until the bananas are soft (a few chunks may remain).

4. Brush beaten egg all around the edges of the pastry ovals with a pastry brush. Put a dollop of cooked banana in the center of each oval, then fold the pastry in half to cover it, and pinch the edges closed to seal them together. Brush the surface with more egg. Cut decorative incisions with a knife. Place the turnovers on a baking sheet and bake about 15 minutes at 355 °F/180 °C.

Orange

13 tbsp/200 g butter, softened
1⅓ cups/200 g confectioners' sugar
5 egg whites
grated rind of 1 orange
1¼ cups/150 g flour, sifted

To finish:
7 oz/200 g fondant
a few drops orange food coloring

Makes: 40 cookies
Preparation time: 20 minutes
Baking time: 15 minutes
Difficulty: ★ ★

With this recipe it will not take long to enjoy the fruits of your labor, as these cookies are simple and quick to make.

If you do not have an electric mixer, the dough can just as easily be beaten with a whisk, provided the butter is softened. The butter and sugar are creamed together, then the egg whites are added little by little, and finally the flour is mixed in with a spatula or wooden spoon.

The dough is squeezed out of a pastry bag onto a baking sheet. This creates evenly sized balls which can then be spread into neat circles simply by tapping the baking sheet.

When the cookies come out of the oven, they should be rolled into cigarillos immediately. If you wait, they will harden and become too crisp for rolling! The rolling stage is not difficult, but does requires deft fingers (avoid using a spoon or other tool; fingers work best) and quick work. The cookies should be wrapped around the handle of a wooden spoon, then slid gently onto a cake rack to cool.

A few precautionary measures should be taken when heating fondant. It should be stirred constantly to maintain a smooth, creamy consistency, and food coloring should be added when the fondant reaches 98.6 °F/37 °C. If it is too thick, a few drops of sugar syrup may be added (see basic recipe).

These ingenious *trompe l'oeil* cookies make a fun dessert for a dinner party or a delicious treat any time.

1. Preheat the oven to 355–375 °F/180–190 °C. Combine the softened butter and sugar in a large mixing bowl and beat with an electric mixer. Add the egg whites little by little, then add the grated orange rind.

2. Continue beating while adding the sifted flour. Grease a baking sheet, fill a pastry bag with the dough, and squeeze dollops the size of a walnut onto the prepared sheet. Tap the baking sheet gently until the balls of dough flatten into even circles. Bake for 15 minutes at 355–375 °F/180–190 °C.

Cigarillos

3. As soon as the cookies come out of the oven, wrap them around the handle of a wooden spoon, then slide onto a cake rack to cool.

4. Dip the tips of each cigarillo into the melted orange fondant (98.6 °F/37 °C). Place on a rack until cool.

Coconut

For the brioche dough:
4 cups/500 g white flour, sifted
2 tsp/10 g salt
3 eggs
3½ tbsp/50 ml water
¼ cup/60 g white sugar
1¾ cups/200 g shredded coconut
¾ oz/20 g compressed fresh yeast
10 tbsp/150 g butter, softened

To finish:
scant ½ cup/50 g shredded coconut
1 egg, lightly beaten

Makes: 10 brioche
Preparation time: 15 minutes
Rising time: 1 hour 30 minutes
Baking time: 15 minutes
Difficulty: ★

Brioche is always delicious, and if the directions are followed with care, these sweet breads will be light, airy and succulent. Brioche are traditionally baked in a distinctive pan with a fluted bottom and a round "head," but they are equally appetizing in other shapes: rolls, braids, or wreaths are also fashioned from brioche dough.

The oven must be preheated to at least 355 °F/180 °C; otherwise the dough will continue to rise while baking and will dry out rather than cooking through. This is true of most breads and pastries which, furthermore, should always be placed on a cake rack to cool as soon as they come out of the oven to allow any steam to evaporate away from the pastry.

The addition of coconut to this classic treat adds an exotic tropical touch. The finished brioche may be dusted with vanilla sugar as well as shredded coconut. Purists may wish to use grated fresh coconut instead of the pre-packaged kind.

One delicious variation for coconut lovers is to add only half the required amount of water, and replace the other half with coconut milk. If canned coconut milk is unavailable, it may be made by simply covering some grated coconut with boiling water. Let it sit for ten minutes, then strain through cheesecloth, reserving the coconut-flavored liquid or "milk."

1. Combine the flour, salt, eggs, water, sugar and shredded coconut in a large mixing bowl. Beat until blended. Then add the yeast and softened butter. Keep beating until the dough pulls away from the sides of the bowl.

2. Shape the dough into a ball, turn it out onto a lightly floured board, cover with a clean, dry cloth, and set aside to rise for 1 hour at room temperature.

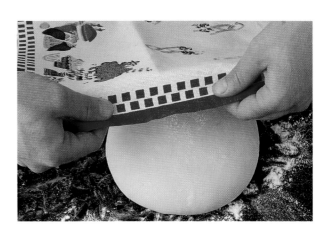

Brioche

3. Divide the dough into pieces weighing about 1¾ oz/50 g each. Shape each piece into a ball, then press down with the side of your hand to form the "head." Place the brioche in greased brioche baking pans, pressing the head down into the larger ball.

4. Set the brioche aside to rise about 30 minutes, until they double in size. To finish, brush the surface with beaten egg. Sprinkle with shredded coconut and bake for 15 minutes at 355 °F/180 °C. Remove from the oven, turn out of the pans and cool on a rack.

Lime

2 cups/250 g rye flour, sifted
1 cup/125 g white flour, sifted
1½ oz/40 g yeast
1 cup/225 ml water
2 tsp/10 g salt
grated rind of 1 lime
½ cup/50 g nigella seeds

Serves	*6*
Preparation time:	*15 minutes*
Rising time:	*1 hour*
Baking time:	*45 minutes*
Difficulty:	★

Rye bread used to be considered "poor people's bread" because paupers were not allowed to have white flour. Rye bread was therefore never seen on banquet tables at receptions or feasts, and was long unknown to the upper classes. Today, rye has come back into fashion, thanks to its rich flavor and high energy and nutritional value. This recipe uses a combination of rye and white flours to make the bread a bit lighter, and the lime adds an agreeable tangy note.

It is best to knead the dough for a long time, at least 15 to 20 minutes, to make sure it incorporates a lot of air. The yeast then has time to take effect, fermenting and creating air pockets that make the bread light and delicious. Wrapped in a cloth, the finished loaf will stay fresh for a week.

Nigella (also known as *kalonji* or *charnusshka*) seeds may be found in Indian or Middle Eastern groceries, or through specialist spice merchants; but if difficult to come by, sesame or poppy seeds, or even freshly ground pepper, may be substituted and sprinkled on the loaves just before baking.

This tasty bread will be excellent served with shellfish, plain sea urchins, broiled crawfish, or spicy Caribbean fish dishes. It is also the perfect bread to accompany a cheese plate.

1. Preheat the oven to 430 °F/220 °C. In a large mixing bowl, combine the rye and white flour with the yeast and water. Knead for about 15 minutes, then add the salt and continue kneading another 5 minutes.

2. Add the grated lime rind and mix just until it is incorporated. Shape the dough into a ball, cover with a clean, dry cloth and let it rise for 1 hour.

Rye Wreaths

3. Shape the dough into long thin loaves (baguettes). Use scissors to snip alternating sides as shown, then shape into wreaths, pinching the ends together. Place on a baking sheet that has been greased and floured or covered with parchment paper.

4. Brush the surface with water and sprinkle the nigella seeds on top. Bake 45 minutes at 430 °F/220 °C.

Mango

For the croissant dough:
1¼ cups/300 ml water
4 cups/500 g flour, sifted
2 tsp/10 g salt
3½ tbsp/50 g sugar
3½ tbsp/50 ml milk
1⅔ cup/400 g butter, softened
⅜ oz/10 g yeast

To finish:
1 egg, lightly beaten
1 small jar mango jam
¾ cup/100 g chopped, roasted hazelnuts

Makes: 25 croissants
Preparation time: 30 minutes
Baking time: 15–20 minutes
Chilling time: 30 minutes
Difficulty: ★ ★

Croissants were invented in 1686 to commemorate the victory of the Austrians over the Turks, who had besieged the Austrian capital. Legend has it that a clever baker decided to "capture the flag" of the invading Turks by taking their crescent moon symbol and making it into a pastry to be devoured. Since that day, croissants have become famous worldwide, not as a symbol of war, but rather as a symbol of love and conviviality.

The yeast should be added as soon as the dough has been well mixed, just before it is rolled out. If the yeast is added too soon, the direct contact with the sugar and salt inhibits its fermenting process.

The key to making successful croissants is the vital folding and rolling phase. The dough should be rolled out, folded over the butter, rolled, then folded in thirds, given a quarter turn, rolled out and folded in thirds again, a process that is repeated several times. The dough must rest in the refrigerator at least ten minutes between each rolling out, as this will make it easier to handle. The butter must be cold when it is added, but it may be beaten with a paddle or rolling pin to make it more malleable and easier to roll into the pastry; it should be as soft as the dough itself.

Any type of jam may be used for glazing the croissants: The more exotic the flavor, the better! The chopped hazelnuts may be replaced with chopped, lightly roasted almonds.

These delightful croissants make a perfect light breakfast or afternoon snack.

1. To make the croissant dough, combine all the ingredients except the butter and yeast in a large mixing bowl and blend with an electric mixer. When the dough is well mixed, add the yeast and blend.

2. Turn the dough onto a lightly floured board, roll it out evenly, and place the butter in the middle. Fold all 4 sides over the butter to the center, then roll out the dough again. Fold in thirds, turn 90 degrees, roll out again, and repeat this process 3 or 4 times, refrigerating the dough between each rolling. Refrigerate the finished dough for about 30 minutes.

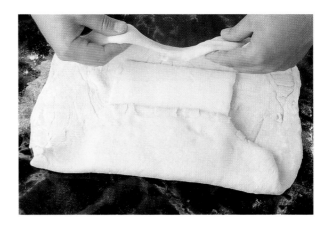

Croissants

3. Preheat the oven to 355 °F/180 °C. Roll the dough out one last time, cut into long bands, then cut each band into isosceles triangles with a base about 3¼ in/8 cm wide. Make a ⅜ in/1 cm cut in the middle of the base side.

4. Roll each triangle, starting at the base, and shape into crescents. Using a pastry brush, brush the top of each croissant with the egg. Place on a non-stick baking sheet, and bake 15–20 minutes at 355 °F/180 °C. When cool, glaze the croissants with warmed jam and sprinkle the chopped nuts on top.

Kiwi-Papaya-Mango

For the cookies:
½ cup/125 g butter
½ cup/125 g sugar
1 egg
2 cups/250 g flour, sifted
1 tbsp baking powder

To finish:
1 small jar kiwi jam
1 small jar papaya jam
1 small jar mango jam
⅔ cup/100 g confectioners' sugar

Makes: 15 cookies
Preparation time: 40 minutes
Baking time: 20 minutes
Chilling time: 1 hour 10 minutes
Difficulty: ★

These elegant cookies are called "dames blanches" (literally "white ladies") for their delicate robes of confectioners' sugar, but their true colors come out in the choice of exotic fruit jams used for the filling.

Pâte sablée is a kind of shortbread dough generally used for cookies of various sizes and shapes. This recipe adds a generous amount of butter for a crisper, lighter effect. The egg is important for the texture of the pastry because it helps unite the butter and sugar, and adds enough moisture to the flour to form a

malleable but firm dough. The egg may be replaced by the same amount of milk, if desired. The baking powder helps the cookies rise; however, baking powder keeps well only about six months, and so is best bought fresh if possible.

When the dough is set aside to rest, it must be covered with plastic wrap to avoid the surface drying out and forming a crust. This cookie dough is rather delicate and must be watched carefully during baking, as it burns easily.

1. In a large mixing bowl, cream the butter and sugar until smooth and fluffy. Add the egg and stir to combine. Then add the flour and baking powder and blend well. Cover and refrigerate for 1 hour.

2. Preheat the oven to 355 °F/180 °C. Turn the dough onto a lightly floured surface, and roll evenly to a thickness of ⅙ in/4 mm. Cut shapes with fluted oval cookie cutters. Cut out a "window," using the same shape but smaller, in the center of half the cookies. Space the cookies well apart on a baking sheet and refrigerate 10 minutes.

"Dames Blanches"

3. Bake the cookies for 20 minutes at 355 °F/180 °C. Cool on a rack, then place a nugget of jam on the center of each whole cookie, using the different flavors as preferred.

4. Dust the "window" cookies generously with confectioners' sugar, then pick them up and lightly drop them just a fraction of an inch, to make any excess sugar fall off. Place a "window" on each cookie base, pressing gently so the jam pops up slightly through the hole.

Hawaiian Chocolate

8¾ oz/250 g dark chocolate
scant 2 cups/235 g flour, sifted
1½ tsp baking powder
a pinch of salt
13 tbsp/200 g butter, softened
1 cup/200 g brown sugar
1 generous cup/100 g shredded coconut
3½ tbsp/50 ml water
1 tsp vanilla extract
3 eggs

Makes: 20 cookies
Preparation time: 20 minutes
Baking time: 20 minutes
Chilling time: 3 hours
Difficulty: ★ ★

The French consider chocolate chip cookies the crowning glory of American baking, and pay homage to Hawaii in this coconut-enhanced tropical version of the classic recipe.

Always use the best quality pure vanilla extract available; avoid poor imitations, which are labeled "vanilla-flavored," The vanilla extract may, however, be replaced by the fresh grainy insides of a vanilla bean, steeped for several hours in the water to be used in the recipe. If freshly shredded coconut is used instead of dried, the amount of water should be cut in half.

For a chunkier chocolate impact, use a block of dark chocolate, refrigerated for at least one hour beforehand to make it easier to chop. Place the cold chocolate on a cutting board and break it up by rolling a rolling pin over it, pressing down firmly. Or you can just use your favorite chocolate chips!

A small ice cream scoop used to place balls of dough on the baking sheet will create cookies with a neat round shape. Each cookie should weigh about 1¾ oz/50 g before baking. They will flatten and spread during baking if the temperature is accurate. However, if the oven is too hot, the outside of the cookies will crisp too quickly and prevent the cookies from flattening. The cookies should be removed from the baking sheet as soon as they come out of the oven, and placed on a rack to cool.

1. Preheat the oven to 355 °F/180 °C. Chop the chocolate and set it aside. Sift together the flour, baking powder and salt. In a large mixing bowl, combine the softened butter with the sugar, shredded coconut and water. Beat until well combined. Stir in the vanilla extract.

2. Add the eggs one by one, mixing thoroughly before adding the sifted dry ingredients.

Chip Cookies

3. Add the chocolate pieces, mix well, and refrigerate for 3 hours.

4. Use an ice cream scoop to make balls of dough evenly spaced on a baking sheet lined with parchment paper. Do not flatten the balls; they will spread naturally during baking. Bake 20 minutes at 355 °F/180 °C. Remove from the oven and cool on a rack.

1⅔ cups/250 g very ripe bananas
2½ cups/300 g flour, sifted
1½ tsp baking powder
a pinch of salt
1¼ cups/250 g dark brown sugar
2 tbsp/30 ml aged rum
6½ tbsp/100 ml milk
⅔ cup/150 ml sunflower oil
2 eggs
1 cup/100 g golden raisins

Serves	*4–6*
Preparation time:	*20 minutes*
Baking time:	*50 minutes*
Difficulty:	*★ ★*

Here is a French Caribbean take on another favorite American recipe. Banana bread is delicious warm or cold, plain or smothered in jam, for breakfast or at teatime. For the sweetest, most intense flavor, the bananas used should be ripe enough to just be turning brown.

The dark brown sugar adds a richness that white sugar simply does not have, but white sugar may be substituted if a pinch of cinnamon is added to it. The golden raisins may be replaced with dark raisins if necessary, but golden raisins look and taste like drops of honey in the sliced bread, and do not seem to be as likely to sink to the bottom during cooking.

The sifted flour should be added to the dough little by little, sprinkled on while beating, to prevent lumps from forming.

Aged rum adds a rich island flavor to the banana bread, but other liqueurs, or simply vanilla extract, may be used if preferred. Taste this enchanting version of banana bread and you may never make it the old way again....

1. Peel and slice the bananas. Using an electric mixer, beat to a pulp in a large mixing bowl.

2. Add the sugar and rum and beat well. Sift together the flour, baking powder and salt; reserve. Grease a loaf pan.

Banana Bread

3. Pour in the milk and mix. Add the oil and then the eggs, one by one, combining well each time. Gradually add the sifted dry ingredients while beating and blend thoroughly.

4. Dust the raisins with a bit of flour before stirring them into the dough. Pour the batter into the prepared pan, and bake about 50 minutes at 320 °F/160 °C. Remove from oven and let cool slightly before removing from the pan. Serve warm or cold.

White Rum

5 eggs, separated
¾ cup/175 g superfine sugar, divided
1 cup/120 g flour, sifted
6½ tbsp/50 g cornstarch
grated rind of 1 lemon and 1 lime
⅓ cup/80 ml white rum

For the cake pan:
5 tsp/25 g butter
5 tsp/25 g granulated sugar

Serves   6–8
Preparation time: 20 minutes
Baking time: 40 minutes
Difficulty: ★

The French word *biscuit* signifies many different variations of moist, light cake, which is leavened either with baking powder or stiffly beaten egg whites, including génoise, Savoy sponge cake, *le roulé, le manqué...*

This recipe adds a tropical twist: white or dark rum from the islands, and lemon and lime zest. Grated orange rind may also be used, but whichever citrus fruit strikes your fancy, it should first be washed, then patted dry before grating. When mixing the dough, only half the flour and cornstarch should be added at one time, to keep it light.

Génoise is the most basic cake in the French pastry chef's repetoire. Its success depends upon beating the egg whites very stiffly, and then folding them very gently into the batter. This preserves the air which has been so carefully whipped in, and hence assures the volume of the finished cake. Whisking the egg yolk mixture until it is very fluffy also lightens the cake and helps it to rise.

Buttering the cake pan and dusting it with superfine or granulated sugar gives the cake an attractive caramel finish. The cake pan should not be filled more than three-quarters full, or the batter may rise too high and overflow. Because this cake is rather delicate, great care should be taken when unmolding it. The cake should be left to cool on a rack until quite cold; then it makes an excellent brunch dish, smothered with jam and served with passion fruit or mint tea.

1. Preheat the oven to 355 °F/180 °C. Whisk the egg yolks with 6½ tbsp/100 g of the sugar in a round-bottomed mixing bowl until the mixture is light and fluffy. Butter a tube cake pan and dust with granulated sugar.

2. Sift together the flour and cornstarch, and add half to the yolk mixture, whisking briskly.

Biscuit

3. Add the dry, grated lemon and lime rind and the rum to the batter. Beat the egg whites with the remaining sugar until stiff.

4. Using a slotted wooden spoon, gently fold half the beaten egg whites into the batter, then add the rest of the flour and cornstarch. Fold in the rest of the beaten whites, then pour the batter into the prepared pan and bake about 40 minutes at 355 °F/180 °C. When done, remove the cake from the pan immediately, and cool on a rack.

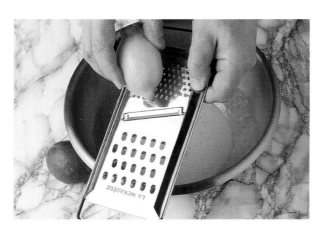

For the batter:
8¾ oz/250 g marzipan
½ cup/50 g candied orange peel
3½ tbsp/50 ml aged rum
3 eggs
a pinch of salt
2½ tbsp/20 g flour, sifted
1½ tsp baking powder
⅓ cup/80 g butter, melted

For the cake pan:
2 tbsp/30 g butter

For the garnish:
confectioners' sugar
a few pieces candied orange peel

Serves	*6–8*
Preparation time:	*25 minutes*
Baking time:	*25 minutes*
Difficulty:	*★*

This cake is a close cousin of the traditional French *pain de Gênes* (literally "Genoese bread") that crossed the Atlantic Ocean to New Orleans a few centuries ago. The treasured age-old recipe is made deliciously rich with the flavor of almond paste, or marzipan, which can be purchased ready-made at most supermarkets.

The candied orange peel, which may be replaced with candied lemon or lime peel, is soaked in rum (or fruit juice for a non-alcoholic version) for extra flavor.

If the batter seems a bit loose, an extra 2½ tbsp/20 g of corn-starch or potato flour, absolutely dry, may be added to make it smooth and give the biscuit a nice grain. The cake pan should not be filled to the top, as the cake could overflow when it rises. Any leftover batter may be baked in small, individual portion cake pans, greased and dusted with flour. To make unmolding easier, the cake pan may be lined with greased parchment paper. The biscuit is ready when a knife inserted near the center comes out clean.

This classic cake is a delicious treat served warm or cold, plain or coated with jam, pastry cream or whipped cream.

1. Preheat the oven to 340 °F/170 °C. Put the marzipan in a large mixing bowl and beat with an electric mixer for about 15 minutes until it has softened to a creamy consistency.

2. Soak the diced, candied orange peel in the rum, reserving a few pieces for decoration. Add the candied peel, rum, eggs, and salt to the softened marzipan, and continue beating until the batter is smooth.

Biscuit

3. Add the flour and baking powder little by little, sprinkling it on the batter while continuing to beat. Then add the warm melted butter and beat a few minutes longer.

4. Grease a fluted cake pan with the solid butter and dust with flour. Fill the pan ¾ full and bake for 25 minutes at 340 °F/170 °C. Remove the cake from the pan while it is still hot. Dust with confectioners' sugar and garnish with the reserved candied orange peel.

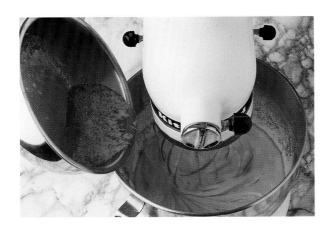

Caribbean

For the batter:
10 tbsp/150 g butter, softened
a pinch of salt
1 cup/150 g confectioners' sugar
3 eggs
3½ tbsp/50 ml orange-flavored liqueur,
    i.e. Shrubb
1½ cups/170 g flour, sifted
1 tsp ground cinnamon
1½ tsp baking powder
¾ cup/100 g chopped pecans
⅓ cup/50 g dark raisins
¾ cup/150 g diced candied fruit

To finish:
1 small jar pineapple jam
a few pieces of candied fruit:
    angelica, maraschino cherries
a few slivered almonds

Serves   6–8
Preparation time: 40 minutes
Baking time: 50 minutes
Difficulty: ★ ★

This delectable fruit cake is easy to make and fun to decorate! Here are a few tricks for best results. First, the butter-sugar-egg mixture should be beaten until it is very smooth and creamy before the flour and baking powder are added. These dry ingredients should be sifted together to prevent lumps. Baking soda may be used instead of baking powder; soda will make the cake rise higher because it creates more fermentation.

If the chopped candied fruit and nuts are dusted in flour before being added to the batter, they will not be so likely to sink to the bottom during baking. To see if the cake is done, insert a knife blade or toothpick into the center. If it comes out clean, then the cake is ready.

Coating the top of the cake with a thin layer of jam gives the cake an appetizing shiny surface and a burst of sweet flavor, though this cake is also delicious without it. For the decoration, the candied cherries should be cut in half and placed face down on the cake. Flower "petals" can be added by placing slivered almonds around the cherries as shown. Candied angelica makes pretty flower "stems." Use your imagination to create other decorations with a personal touch.

This cake can be made several days ahead of time, as it keeps very well simply wrapped in a clean, dry cloth.

1. preheat the oven to 390 °F/200 °C. Beat the butter, salt and sugar in a large mixing bowl. Stir in the eggs one at a time, then add the liqueur and continue beating until the batter is smooth.

2. Sift together the flour, cinnamon and baking powder, then add to the batter and blend well. Roll the chopped pecans, raisins and diced candied fruit in flour, then add to the batter, distributing them well. Pour into a greased, floured loaf pan.

Cake

3. Bake about 50 minutes at 340 °F/170 °C. When done, remove the cake from the pan immediately and let cool on a rack. Use a pastry brush to glaze the top with a thin layer of heated pineapple jam.

4. Decorate the cake with the candied cherries, angelica, and slivered almonds. Serve cold.

2 cups/250 g white flour
⅜ oz/10 g yeast
1⅓ cups/250 g peeled papaya
1½ tsp/8 g salt

Serves	*4–6*
Preparation time:	*20 minutes*
Rising time:	*30 minutes*
Baking time:	*15–20 minutes*
Difficulty:	★

This bread is a daring blend of ordinary bread dough with exotic fruit, and it is a wild success! The papaya retains both its fragrance and its flavor during baking, resulting a distinctive and delicious fruit-scented rolls.

The bread's rich texture comes from proper kneading: The dough should be very smooth and well-blended, easily done with an electric mixer, but perfectly feasible by hand as long as you apply a little elbow grease.

In this recipe, juicy papaya fruit replaces the water that is normally used in bread dough. Guava or mango flesh could be used instead, for a sweeter variation.

This bread needs to be baked at a high temperature, so the oven must be preheated for at least 10 minutes to ensure that the crust sets quickly, which prevents the inside from drying out. It is advisable to place a small dish of water in the oven, creating a moister heat than that provided by most home ovens. This additional moisture gives the crust a deep golden amber color. Another way to achieve this is to splash a glass of hot water on the bottom of the oven during baking.

1. Combine the flour and yeast in a large mixing bowl.

2. Peel the papaya, remove and set aside the seeds, purée the flesh in a blender or food processor, then add the papaya and seeds to the flour. Beat on high speed, adding the salt while beating. The dough is ready when it is perfectly blended and pulls away cleanly from the sides of the bowl.

Bread

3. Turn the dough onto a lightly floured board, shape it into a large ball, cover with a clean, dry cloth and set aside to rise at room temperature for about 30 minutes. Then knead the dough again, divide and shape it into small balls, and place on a non-stick baking sheet.

4. Bake 15–20 minutes at 340 °F/170 °C with a dish of water in the bottom of the oven. Place the rolls on a rack to cool.

Exotic Four

For the batter:
5 large eggs (10½ oz/300 g total),
  separated
1¼ cups/300 g sugar, divided
2½ cups/300 g flour, sifted
1 tbsp baking powder
1¼ cups/300 g butter, melted
¾ cup/150 g diced candied fruit
3½ tbsp/50 ml white rum

For the cake pan:
2 tbsp/30 g butter
¼ cup/30 g flour

Serves	6–8
Preparation time:	25 minutes
Baking time:	25 minutes
Difficulty:	★

Served warm or cold, whatever colors and flavors of candied fruit are chosen, the Four Quarter Cake is a reliable standby, easy and delicious.

A kitchen scale is an essential tool in every French chef's kitchen, and should be used, if possible, for best results in recreating these recipes. Odd as it may seem, the eggs should be weighed whole in their shell. The Four Quarter Cake depends on exactly equal quantities (by weight) of the four major ingredients, so this extra trouble is a minor concession to make the cake a major success. Standard U.S. large eggs weigh 2 oz /60 g apiece in the shell, and so will work in this recipe even if a kitchen scale is not available.

Another key to success is folding the beaten egg whites into the batter very gently to retain as much air and volume as possible. The diced fruit should be dusted in flour before being added to the batter, to prevent it from sinking to the bottom during baking. To allow extra moisture to evaporate away from the cake, it should be removed from the pan fresh from the oven and left on a rack to cool.

This simple cake is wonderful served with mango or papaya jam, accompanied by a cold glass of fruit juice, and will soon become a standard in your repertoire.

1. Preheat the oven to 355 °F/180 °C. Butter a square cake pan and dust with flour. Place the egg yolks in a large mixing bowl. Add 1 cup/250 g of the sugar and whisk them until pale yellow.

2. Add the flour, baking powder and melted butter to the yolks and sugar. Mix well. Soak the diced candied fruit in the rum.

Quarter Cake

3. Add the fruit and rum to the batter and stir. Beat the egg whites with the remaining sugar until stiff.

4. Fold the beaten egg whites into the batter, then turn it into the prepared pan and bake at 355 °F/180 °C about 25 minutes. Remove the cake from the pan as soon as it comes out of the oven. Cool on a rack. Serve cold.

Saint John's

For the vanilla batter:
¾ cup/90 g flour, sifted
1½ tsp baking powder
2½ tbsp/30 g cornstarch
4 eggs, separated
½ cup plus 2 tbsp/150 g sugar, divided
3½ tbsp/50 g butter, melted
½ tsp ground cinnamon
1 vanilla bean or ½ tsp vanilla extract
grated rind of 1 lime

For the chocolate batter:
6½ tbsp/50 g flour
½ tbsp/baking powder
2½ tbsp/30 g cornstarch
2½ tbsp/30 g unsweetened cocoa powder
4 eggs, separated
½ cup plus 2 tbsp/150 g sugar, divided
3½ tbsp/50 g butter, melted

Serves	6–8
Preparation time:	45 minutes
Baking time:	35 minutes
Difficulty:	★

Saint John's cake is a succulent marbled vanilla and chocolate cake, spiked with a burst of lime and the exotic spice of your choice. Cinnamon is used here, but anise, nutmeg, or cardamom would be equally interesting choices. This cake can be made in any shape pan and is perfect for after-school snacks.

For adult consumption, aged rum, brandy or Licor 43 (vanilla-flavored liqueur) may be added to the vanilla batter instead of the lime and cinnamon. Orange liqueur, crème de cacao, or any other liqueur that harmonizes well with chocolate may be used in the chocolate batter. Real vanilla beans lend an incomparable heady fragrance, but if they are hard to find pure vanilla extract works well; just avoid the ersatz extract which is labeled "vanilla-flavored."

In this illustration the chocolate and vanilla batters are simply layered, but a marbled look can be created by gently swirling the two batters with a spoon. The visual effect will be noticed and appreciated once the cake has been baked and sliced. Enjoy!

1. Preheat the oven to 355 °F/180 °C. To make the vanilla batter, sift together the flour, baking powder and cornstarch. Beat the egg yolks and 6½ tbsp/100 g of the sugar in a large mixing bowl until fluffy and pale yellow. Stir in the dry ingredients, then add the melted butter and blend well.

2. Add the cinnamon and the content of the vanilla bean (or the extract), then the lime rind. Mix well. Beat the egg whites and the remaining sugar until stiff. Fold the whites into the batter.

Cake

3. Make the chocolate batter in the same way, but sift the cocoa powder with the other dry ingredients and omit the vanilla, cinnamon and lime.

4. Grease and dust a cake pan. Pour the vanilla batter into the cake pan. Fill a pastry bag with the chocolate batter and squeeze it into the vanilla batter, or simply spoon it in. Swirl the batters slightly for a marbled effect, if desired. Bake about 35 minutes at 355 °F/180 °C. Remove from the cake pan while still hot and cool on a rack.

6½ tbsp/100 g butter
⅓ cup plus 1 tsp/85 ml water
¾ cup/150 g brown sugar
14 oz/400 g dark chocolate, chopped
2 eggs
1 tsp vanilla extract
¾ cup plus 1 tbsp/100 g flour, sifted
½ tsp/2 g baking powder
a pinch of salt
½ cup/100 g diced, candied papaya
1 cup/150 g chopped walnuts

Serves	*4–6*
Preparation time:	*25 minutes*
Baking time:	*40–45 minutes*
Chilling time:	*2 hours*
Difficulty:	★

That ultimate American dessert, brownies, is here reinvented by a French chef who adds a tropical twist and calls it Key West in honor of his unforgettable vacation in that island paradise.

These brownies are easy to make, and the luscious combination of chocolate, vanilla, nuts and papya goes well à la mode with vanilla ice cream, or simply with afternoon tea.

When cooking the sugar, water and butter, the pot should be watched carefully to make sure the mixture does not caramelize. As soon as it boils, it is poured over half the chocolate, the rest having been chopped and set aside to be mixed in at the end. To save preparation time, good quality chocolate chips may be used instead.

The candied papaya, diced small for a more discrete flavor, may be replaced with finely chopped candied orange peel, pineapple, mandarines or any other exotic candied fruit that appeals to you.

The brownies should be left in the pan to cool, then refrigerated for two hours before being cut into squares. Though it may be difficult to persuade chocolate-lovers to wait so long, this allows the chocolate chips to harden, and makes it easier to achieve neatly sliced edges. Try cutting the brownies into diamonds or other elegant shapes, and use your imagination to create an impressive presentation.

1. Preheat the oven to 340 °F/170 °C. Melt the butter, water and sugar in a heavy-bottomed pot. Bring to a boil. Put half the chopped chocolate in a large mixing bowl, and reserve the other half.

2. Pour the boiling mixture over the bowl of chocolate, and blend with an electric mixer. Add the eggs one by one, then the vanilla extract, flour, baking powder and salt. Combine thoroughly.

Brownies

3. Add the diced papaya, remaining chocolate chips, and the chopped walnuts. Stir gently.

4. Butter a square cake pan and line the bottom with parchment paper. Pour the batter into the pan and bake 40–45 minutes at 340 °F/170 °C. Let the brownies cool before removing from the pan. Refrigerate for 2 hours, then cut.

For the dough:
1¼ cups/300 ml water
4 cups/500 g flour
2 tbsp/10 g salt
3½ tbsp/50 g sugar
3½ tbsp/50 ml milk
⅜ oz/10 g yeast
1¾ cups/400 g butter
1 egg, lightly beaten

For the pastry cream filling:
  (see basic recipe)
4 vanilla beans
2 cups/500 ml milk
3 eggs
½ cup/125 g sugar
6½ tbsp/50 g cornstarch

For the syrup:
  (see basic recipe)
3½ tbsp/50 g sugar
3½ tbsp/50 ml water
3½ tbsp/50 ml dark rum

To finish:
1 cup/100 g slivered almonds, lightly
  roasted

Makes: 25 small croissants
Preparation time: 45 minutes
Rising time: 30 minutes
Baking time: 15–20 minutes
Difficulty: ★ ★

Breakfast in bed with croissants: what a treat! Homemade croissants are sheer luxury, and their taste is beyond compare. Croissants require a bit of work, but once you have tried these you may never go back to the store-bought variety!

To make perfect croissants, a few rules should be observed: First, when mixing the dough, the beater should be on slow speed to gently blend the water, milk, sugar and flour. Once the dough begins to take shape, increase the speed slightly and add the yeast. If the yeast is added too soon, direct contact with the sugar may inhibit its rising power. The yeast should be blended for a few minutes before the dough is rolled out.

The dough must be rolled out and folded several times; it may be refrigerated and left to rest longer than 10 minutes each time if that is convenient. The butter should be cool but pliable, about the same texture as the dough. This allows it to spread evenly between the layers of dough without melting, giving the finished croissants their characteristic rich buttery taste and tender, flaky texture.

This is truly the classic French *grandmere's* recipe, and is equally wonderful served plain, coated with an exotic fruit jam, or filled with cinnamon—or passion fruit—flavored pastry cream. Once the croissants have been filled, the tops may be glazed and garnished with lightly roasted slivered almonds. Other chopped, roasted nuts may be used instead; for example, pine nuts, hazelnuts, or even toasted shredded coconut.

1. Combine the water, flour, salt, sugar and milk in a large bowl and beat on slow speed. When well mixed, add the yeast. Beat at higher speed a few minutes. Turn the dough onto a lightly floured board and roll out a large rectangle. Place the softened butter in the middle. Fold all 4 sides into the center, covering the butter. Roll out the pastry again, then fold in thirds, turn 90 degrees, and roll out again. Repeat this process 3 times, refrigerating the dough between "turns."

2. The last time the pastry is rolled out, cut the large rectangle into long bands about 6 in/15 cm wide, then cut isosceles triangles with a base side about 3¼ in/8 cm long. Make a ⅜ in/1 cm cut in the center of the base, and roll each croissant from the base. Curve each into a crescent shape, then brush the top with beaten egg. Place on a non-stick baking sheet and let rest at room temperature 30 minutes.

Filled Croissants

3. Preheat the oven to 355 °F/180 °C. Make the pastry cream according to the basic recipe, infusing the vanilla beans in the milk. When finished, whisk the cream briskly and set aside. Bake the croissants 15–20 minutes at 355 °F/180 °C.

4. When the croissants have cooled on a rack, cut them in half (use an electric carving knife for a cleaner cut). Make the sugar syrup (see basic recipe) with the rum and let it cool. Dip the croissant halves into the cold syrup. Fill a pastry bag with the pastry cream and cover each croissant base. Then put the top halves back on and brush with a thin layer of jam. Garnish with the almonds.

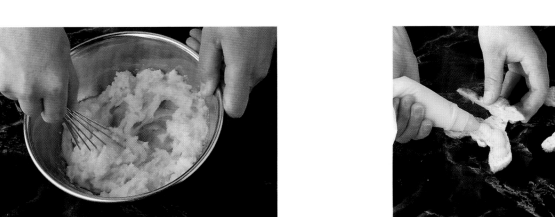

⅔ cup/100 g peeled, diced pineapple
1⅔ cups/200 g peeled, grated carrots
1 cup/200 g brown sugar
3 eggs
1 drop vanilla extract
⅔ cup/150 ml sunflower oil
2½ cups/300 g flour

1 tbsp baking powder
½ tsp/2 g ground cinnamon
¼ tsp/1 g ginger powder
¼ tsp/1 g ground cloves
a pinch of salt
3½ oz/100 g dark chocolate

Makes: 12 large muffins
Preparation time: 30 minutes
Baking time: 25–30 minutes
Difficulty: ★

These muffins are in honor of all plantation farmers—cane sugar, pineapple and carrot planters—and the fruits of their labor. The mixture of fruit and vegetables is healthful and nourishing, while the addition of sugar and spice makes these muffins very flavorful indeed.

This mixture of sweet vegetable and spice creates an unusual cross between two old favorites: gingerbread and carrot cake. The choice of spices may be varied to suit your taste. Carrots are one of the sweetest vegetables and combine well with the sweet acidity of the pineapple, but other juicy fruits such as cherimoyas or mangos may be substituted.

This recipe is adapted to make muffins or cupcakes, but any interestingly shaped individual portion pans will serve as well. The batter should not be filled to the brim in any pan, however, as it will rise quite a bit during baking. If a miniature muffin is desired, then the baking time must be reduced by half. If a large cake pan or loaf pan is used instead, then add approximately 20 minutes to the baking time. A cake may be served in slices.

To check if the muffins are finished baking, slide the tip of a knife into the center of one; if it comes out clean and dry, the muffins are ready.

1. Preheat the oven to 340 °F/170 °C. Combine the diced pineapple and grated carrots with the sugar in a large mixing bowl and beat with an electric mixer.

2. Add the eggs, vanilla extract, and oil, and continue beating.

Muffins

3. Add the flour, baking powder, cinnamon, ginger, ground cloves, and salt. Continue mixing until the batter is smooth and well-blended.

4. Using a pastry bag or a spoon, fill each muffin cup ¾ full with batter. Bake 25–30 minutes at 340 °F/170 °C. Allow to cool before serving with morsels of dark chocolate.

Cinnamon

a waffle iron

For the waffle batter:
1 cup plus 2 tbsp/275 ml milk, divided
10 tbsp/150 g butter, divided
1 cup/125 g flour
1 cup/100 g confectioners' sugar, divided
4 eggs
⅔ cup/150 ml heavy cream
½ tsp ground cinnamon or orange-flower
  water
grated rind of 1 orange

To finish:
confectioners' sugar
sweet cocoa powder (optional)

Makes: 8–10 waffles
Preparation time: 15 minutes
Baking time: 4–5 minutes per
    waffle
Difficulty: ★

A waffle iron certainly makes it easier to prepae these delicious treats, especially to create the traditional shape and distinctive texture: crispy on the outside, soft and tender on the inside. But if an iron is not available, waffles can still be made using an ordinary pie pan; just spread the batter evenly and bake for five to six minutes.

Waffle batter needs to be prepared in a pot over high heat, stirring constantly to remove as much moisture as possible. This should be done quickly, until the batter no longer sticks to the sides of the pot. Then the cream and milk may be added

without forming lumps. The waffles benefit if the batter is left to rest for an hour or so before cooking the waffles.

This recipe uses cinnamon for a hint of exotic flavor, but orange-flower water makes a lovely variation and complements the orange rind as well.

The waffles may be served as a dessert dusted with confectioners' sugar or sweet cocoa powder, or garnished with whipped cream or exotic fruit jam. These scrumptious honeycomb-shaped treats are also delicious served with honey or maple syrup for brunch.

1. Combine ¾ cup/175 g milk with 3½ tbsp/50 g butter in a pot and bring to a boil. When the butter has melted, remove from the heat and add the flour and half the sugar. Return to high heat and stir constantly with a wooden spoon until the mixture pulls cleanly away from the sides of the pan.

2. Pour the mixture into a large mixing bowl. Using the kneading hook of an electric mixer, beat on medium speed, adding the eggs one by one and then the remaining sugar. Mix until well-blended.

Orange Waffles

3. Replace the kneading hook with the beater attachment and continue beating. Gradually add the cream and remaining milk, then the cinnamon and grated orange rind. Preheat the waffle iron.

4. Melt the remaining butter and use a pastry brush to paint the entire surface of the waffle iron, top and bottom. Ladle some batter into the waffle iron and cook for 4–5 minutes. When the waffles are done, dust with confectioners' sugar or sweet cocoa powder and serve warm.

For the batter:
1⅓ cups/250 g finely ground almonds
3 cups/450 g confectioners' sugar, sifted
8¾ oz/250 g egg whites (whites of 8 large
   eggs)
3½ tbsp/50 g granulated sugar

To finish:
a few drops of yellow and green food
   coloring
a few drops of grenadine syrup
1 small jar guava jam
1 small jar banana jam
1 small jar coconut jam

Makes: 40 macaroons
Preparation time: 20 minutes
Baking time: 15–20 minutes
Difficulty: ★

There is a legend about macaroons dating back to the 8th century, when they were made in monasteries: The macaroons were said to be made in the shape of monks' navels. Although the Carmelite nuns who made the macaroons had fled society, they apparently knew something about life in the outside world!

The mixture of finely ground almonds and sifted confectioners' sugar must be perfectly dry. Any moisture will cause the macaroons to crack during baking. To ensure success, the mixture can be placed in front of an open oven door to dry.

A wide range of jams will make delicious "glue" to fill the macaroon sandwiches; experiment to find the best combination of flavors. The batter is colored red, yellow and green to indicate each type. Other flavors may also be added to the batter; for example, vanilla extract would go well with guava macaroons, and ground pistachios could complement the banana macaroons. Cocoa powder would enhance coconut macaroons.

Sometimes macaroons do not come out as smooth and shiny as they should, but do not worry: The inside will still be soft and delicious. When they have baked, slide the parchment paper onto a moist surface and the macaroons will slip off easily. Despite their sinful sweetness, macaroons are packed with redeeming food value: Egg whites are low in fat but high in protein, and almonds are full of fiber, vitamins and minerals. Macaroons make a light, tasty and nutritious snack any time.

1. Preheat the oven to 300 °F/150 °C. Blend the finely ground almonds and sifted confectioners' sugar in a large mixing bowl with a whisk. In a another mixing bowl, beat the egg whites and sugar until stiff. Then gently fold the whites into the almond mixture.

2. Divide the batter into 3 different bowls, and add a different food coloring or syrup to each bowl. Use a pastry bag to squeeze macaroons onto a baking sheet lined with parchment paper.

Macaroons

3. Bake for 25–30 minutes at 300 °F/150 °C. As soon as the macaroons come out of the oven, remove them from the paper by sprinkling a little water under the paper. Cool on a rack.

4. Glue 2 macaroons together by placing a tiny spoonful of jam on the flat bottom of one cookie, then gently pressing another onto it. Continue, using all 3 flavors of jam.

Bougoulou

1 cup/250 g butter, softened
1⅓ cups/250 g confectioners' sugar
4 eggs
3 cups/375 g flour, sifted
½ tsp vanilla extract
1⅓ cups/150 g shredded coconut

To finish:
scant 1 cup/100 g shredded coconut
3½ oz/100 g tempered dark chocolate

Makes: 30 cookies
Preparation time: 20 minutes
Baking time: 20 minutes
Difficulty: ★

These cookies are child's play to make; in fact, children will love helping to make as well as eat them!

It is also easy to vary the flavors by improvising different combinations. Ground hazelnuts or almonds may be substituted for the coconut. Vanilla extract is the main flavoring in these cookies, but it may be replaced by cinnamon, ground cardamom or even nutmeg.

Shredded coconut is readily available in stores, but it is fun to make your own. A fresh coconut must first be cracked open. The white flesh is grated finely, then dried under a broiler.

The cookies should be watched closely during baking, as they tend to burn easily. If the tops start to brown too soon, the cookies may be covered with a sheet of tin foil to allow time to bake thoroughly without burning.

Once the cookies have cooled, coat the tops with dark chocolate that has been melted in a double boiler. The chocolate should be melted until just barely hot, no more than 89.6–91.4 °F/32–33 °C, in order to avoid turning dull.

These cookies look tempting arranged by alternating colors, dancing the Bougoulou on an elegant serving plate.

1. Preheat the oven to 320 °F/160 °C. To make the cookie dough, combine the softened butter and sugar in a large bowl and beat until creamy and light.

2. Add the eggs one by one, blending between each addition, then stir in the flour and vanilla. Beat until the dough is smooth and creamy.

Cookies

3. Add the shredded coconut and blend. Grease a baking sheet or use a non-stick baking sheet.

4. Use a pastry bag to squeeze the dough onto the baking sheet. Sprinkle some extra coconut on each cookie, then bake 20 minutes at 320 °F/160 °C. Melt the chocolate in a double boiler and dip the tops of half of the cooled cookies into it. Sprinkle more shredded coconut on top. Set aside to cool.

Almond Pineapple

For the cookies:
1 cup/250 g sugar
1⅓ cups/250 g finely ground almonds
5¼ oz/150 g egg whites (whites of
    5 large eggs)
2½ tbsp/50 g guava jam or 3½ tbsp/50 ml
    guava juice

To finish:
⅓ cup/50 g blanched almonds
⅔ cup/100 g pine nuts
1 cup/100 g shelled pecans
1 small jar pineapple jam

Makes:	*20 cookies*
Preparation time:	*45 minutes*
Baking time:	*15 minutes*
Resting time:	*24 hours*
Difficulty:	★

The warm tropical sweetness of these cookies will melt away a dreary, rainy day and bring sunshine to the faces of those who taste them. In fact, baking these cookies is a perfect rainy day acitivity with children, who can be allowed a free hand in shaping and decorating them with various nuts or dried fruit.

The blanched almonds and the whole nuts are used for the garnish; if you run out, they can be replaced with others, such as walnuts or hazelnuts.

The dough may be divided into several parts, and each part flavored differently, one with vanilla, one with cinnamon, one with orange-flower water, and so on.

It is vital that the dough be left to rest for 24 hours, preferably in a cool place. This gives the cookies a better consistency and gives the flavors time to develop fully. For an appetizing, glossy finish, the jam glaze should be brushed on when the cookies first come out of the oven. If the jam is first heated with a little water to make it more liquid, it will be easy to paint on with a pastry brush.

These cookies may be made several days in advance; they will keep perfectly in a dry, airtight container, unless they are immediately devoured!

1. Combine the sugar and finely ground almonds in a large mixing bowl and beat with an electric mixer on slow speed.

2. Slowly add the egg whites and increase the speed.

Guava Petits Fours

3. Pour in the guava juice and beat until the dough is soft and smooth. Wet your hands and shape the dough into small balls. Then flatten the balls into crescent shapes or ovals, if desired.

4. Roll the crescent shapes in the pine nuts, press the blanched almonds on the ovals and the pecans on the balls, and place the cookies on a baking sheet. Set aside in a cool place for 24 hours. Then bake 15 minutes at 428 °F/220 °C. When the cookies have cooled, paint the tops with warm pineapple jam.

Curry

4 cups/500 g flour, sifted
1¼ cups/300 ml water
⅜ oz/10 g yeast
2 tsp/10 g salt
scant ½ cup/100 g curry powder

For the decoration:
4 tsp/20 g curry powder

Makes:	*20 small rolls*
Preparation time:	*20 minutes*
Rising time:	*1 hour*
Baking time:	*15 minutes*
Difficulty:	★

Wheat has been cultivated for thousands of years, and people have learned to use it in myriad ways. Wheat probably originated in Asia, and the Spaniards brought it to the New World in the 16th century. It has long been a staple on every continent.

Grains of wheat are round, ranging in color from golden-yellow to light and dark brown. There are many varieties, grouped in three main categories: soft, hard, and semi-hard. Most flour is made of soft wheat, including the best quality baking flour, because it contains the most starch and pliable, elastic gluten. For best results, look for bread flour or high-gluten flour; or buy gluten separately (at natural food stores) and mix a spoonful into your ordinary flour before baking.

This is a classic recipe made exotic with curry. Vary the flavor by using different curry blends, such as cardamom or garam masala. For best results, mix your favorite combination of spices and grind them freshly in a spice grinder or small coffee mill. If using store-bought curry powder, be sure it is fresh and fragrant; if it smells dusty, the bread will taste similar!

One baker's trick that applies to all bread-making is that the salt should not be in direct contact with the yeast, as it kills the live yeast organisms that make bread rise.

These bread rolls keep for a few days wrapped in a clean, dry cloth. They will go well with any curry dish, a plate of salad and cheese, or topped by a slice of ham.

1. Combine the flour, water and yeast in a large mixing bowl, and beat on slow speed for about 15 minutes. Then add the salt and curry and increase the mixer speed. Continue beating another 5 minutes.

2. Shape the dough into a ball, cover with a clean, dry cloth and let rise at room temperature for about 30 minutes. Turn the dough onto a lightly floured board, divide into pieces of about 1¾ oz/50 g each, and shape into balls.

Rolls

3. Place the dough balls on a non-stick baking sheet and let them rise for about 30 minutes. Then use scissors to cut a cross in the top of each roll.

4. Sprinkle some curry on each roll, and bake about 15 minutes at 465 °F/240 °C.

Shrubb

1¼ cups/300 g butter, softened
1 cup/250 g sugar
2 eggs
5 tbsp/75 ml milk
3½ tbsp/50 ml orange-flavored liqueur,
   i.e. Shrubb
4 cups/500 g flour, sifted
1 tbsp baking powder
6½ tbsp/50 g cornstarch

To finish:
½ cup/100 g various candied fruit
   (maraschino cherries, angelica, citron,
   melon, etc)

Makes: 40 cookies
Preparation time: 40 minutes
Baking time: 20 minutes
Difficulty: ★

Candied fruit have been used in baking at least as far back as the Middle Ages, when they were used in pâtes as well as cakes. The medieval palate used sweetmeats as generously as it could, often in combinations we would consider odd today, and so candied fruit might be used as we would use spices; indeed, the French called them *epices de chamber* or "chamber spices."

Candied fruit are wonderful as decoration because of the range of bright colors: the green of angelica, the red of cherries, the pale green of citron and the yellow of melon. The choices are endless, so be as creative as you like.

These cookies are flavored with Shrubb, a rum-based orange liqueur, but other orange-flavored liqueurs, or simply orange juice, can also be used. In this recipe it is important that the flour be sifted with the baking powder and cornstarch to avoid any lumps in the dough. The fruit should be gently pressed down into the surface of the cookies so it will stick long after baking. Once the cookies have cooled, they may be painted with exotic fruit jam to give them a delicious, elegant glaze.

These cookies may be made several days ahead, provided they are stored in a dry, airtight container. They are excellent whether served in great quantities on buffet tables or simply for tea with friends.

1. Cream the butter and sugar in the mixing bowl of an electric mixer, then add the eggs one by one, then the milk and liqueur. Blend until the dough is nice and smooth.

2. Sift together the flour, baking powder, and cornstarch and add them to the dough, stirring just until the ingredients are combined.

Sugar Cookies

3. Use a pastry bag with a fluted nozzle to squeeze the dough in an S-shape or round shape onto a non-stick baking sheet.

4. Decorate each cookie with diced pieces of candied fruit, pressing the fruit gently into the dough. Bake 20 minutes at 320 °F/160 °C. Allow the cookies to cool before removing them from the baking sheet. Serve cold.

½ watermelon
1 cantaloupe
1 kiwi
1 small jar guava jelly

For the short pastry:
  (see basic recipe)
⅓ cup/50 g confectioners' sugar
1 egg
a pinch of salt
½ cup/125 g butter
1 vanilla bean
2 tbsp water
2 cups/250 g flour, sifted

For the pastry cream:
  (see basic recipe)
4 vanilla beans
2 cups/500 ml milk
3 eggs
½ cup/125 g sugar
6½ tbsp/50 g cornstarch
3½ tbsp/50 ml lychee liqueur
3½ tbsp/50 ml passion fruit liqueur
3½ tbsp/50 ml grenadine syrup

Makes:	30 small tarts
Preparation time:	40 minutes
Baking time:	15 minutes
Difficulty:	★

Mambo

These colorful little tarts are easy and enjoyable to make, and as appealing to the palate as they are to the eye!

If hard, high-gluten flour is perfect for bread, it is disastrous for tender cakes and pastry doughs like this one. Use the softest white flour you can find for pastry dough; cake flour or brands milled in the southern U.S. are best.

Short pastry is an easy-to-handle dough that is used for most tart shells and pie crusts. Without sugar, the same pastry is perfect for savory pies and quiches; however, the butter should then be replaced with oil, and the amount of water slightly reduced. The pastry may be made the day before baking and set aside in the refrigerator covered with a clean, damp cloth. It should be removed from the refrigerator about 15 minutes before use.

The fruit may be varied depending on the season and your fancy, but it should have a firm flesh that can be scooped with a melon baller. The lychee and passion fruit liqueurs and grenadine syrup are combined with the pastry cream for added flavor and color; other liqueurs may be substituted as preferred.

A certain deftness of hand and eye for color are needed for garnishing the tartlets, as the fruit balls are tiny, and the filling can be messy. The fruit colors should be alternated for the most aesthetic, artistic effect.

1. Make the short pastry according to the basic recipe, but using the ingredients listed above. Roll it out thinly and evenly. Use pastry cutters to cut out the pastry, and line each tartlet pan with the dough.

2. Make tiny fruit balls using a small melon baller, and set aside.

Tartlets

3. Fill each tartlet shell with baking weights or dried beans and bake 15 minutes at 390 °F/200 °C. Make the pastry cream (see basic recipe), then divide it evenly among 3 bowls. Add one liqueur to each bowl and stir. Then use a pastry bag to squeeze some cream into each pre-baked tartlet shell.

4. Garnish the tartlets with the fruit balls. Warm the guava jelly and brush it on the tartlets with a pastry brush.

6 eggs
¼ cup/60 ml milk
1¼ cups/300 g sugar
3 cups/375 g flour, sifted
1½ tbsp/15 g baking powder
grated rind of ½ lime
grated rind of ½ orange
1 cup/250 g butter, softened
1 small jar orange marmalade

Serves	8
Preparation time:	20 minutes
Chilling time:	2–3 hours
Baking time:	20 minutes
Difficulty:	★

These little cakes were immortalized by the renowned French author, Marcel Proust, when he wrote of "short, plump cakes that seem to have been baked in scallop shells." Proust went on to describe them as "gorgeous little seashells of pastry, so buttery and sensual beneath their austere and pious pleating." Thanks to the nostalgic, poetical waxing of this prince of the French language, madeleines have become the most celebrated cakes in literature.

This recipe is unique in its addition of citrus flavors, but has been perfectly adapted for success. As always in baking, the ingredients must be weighed and measured scrupulously to avoid disappointment. A special mold is traditionally used to bake madeleines, though muffin cups will do, if necessary.

The citrus flavor is added in the form of grated zest. Avoid using fruit juice at all costs, as this would make the dough too liquid and would prevent it from rising during baking. The citrus rind may be varied according to preference.

The dough may be prepared the day before and kept in the refrigerator. If the dough is made the same day, it should be chilled for at least two to three hours.

One hour before baking, remove the dough from the refrigerator and stir it with a spatula. The dough should turn light in color while the consistency remains fairly thick. Madeleines will keep well for several days in an airtight container. One bite of these and you will know why Proust never forgot them....

1. Break the eggs into a large mixing bowl and whisk, gradually adding the milk. Then add the sugar and continue beating briskly.

2. Sift the flour into the mixture, then the baking powder, and blend well. Add the grated lime rind and orange rind. Finally, add the softened butter and whisk thoroughly.

Madeleines

3. Carefully butter the madeleine pan with softened butter, using a pastry brush.

4. Refrigerate the dough for at least 2 hours, then stir. Preheat the oven to 355 °F/180 °C. Spoon the dough into the madeleine pan filling each cup only ⅔ full. Bake for 20 minutes at 355 °F/180 °C. The madeleines may be served plain or filled with orange marmalade.

Kiwi Mango

For the puff pastry:
(see basic recipe)
2 cups/250 g flour, sifted
13 tbsp/200 g butter
1 tsp/5 g salt
⅔ cup/150 ml water

For the pastry cream:
(see basic recipe)
4 vanilla beans
2 cups/500 ml milk
3 eggs
½ cup/125 g sugar
6½ tbsp/50 g cornstarch
3½ tbsp/50 ml passion fruit liqueur
3½ tbsp/50 ml dark rum

To finish:
2 kiwis
1 mango
confectioners' sugar
3½ oz/100 g fondant
3 tbsp/20 g chopped, roasted almonds
1 small jar mango jam

Makes: 40 petits fours
Preparation time: 40 minutes
Baking time: 15 minutes
Difficulty: ★ ★

Millefeuille literally means "thousand leaves," and refers to the tender, flaky layers of the best puff pastry. As a *petit four*, or bite-size morsel of cake, millefeuille is a classic combination of puff pastry, pastry cream and icing. They have been famous in pastry for over a century, and deservedly so, as they can be enjoyed in so many variations. In this recipe they are filled with pastry cream flavored with rum or passion fruit liqueur, but the filling may be flavored with different juices or liqueurs to complement the choice of topping.

Puff pastry is not too difficult to make, but if time is short it may be purchased frozen, ready to cut and bake. A chef's trick to achieve nice flat sheets of baked puff pastry is to prick it all over with a fork before baking.

These petits fours should be assembled as follows: Use a pastry bag to squeeze a layer of plain pastry cream onto some of the puff pastry rectangles. Place a second layer of puff pastry on top of the cream, followed by a second layer of cream. Finally, set a third layer of puff pastry on top, and dust it with confectioners' sugar. The same process is repeated for all the puff pastry shapes, with the addition of a top layer of fondant or thinly sliced fruit on some.

The millefeuilles may be iced with fondant and chopped, roasted almonds, or glazed with mango jam, or simply dusted with confectioners' sugar. These pastries are fragile and must be handled with care. Refrigerate before serving with a fruit juice cocktail or a glass of good champagne.

1. Make the puff pastry according to the basic recipe, using the amounts above. Roll it out thinly and evenly and place on a baking sheet covered with parchment paper. Prick it all over with a fork, then cover with a second baking sheet and bake 15 minutes at 355 °F/180 °C. When cold, use a very sharp knife or electric carving knife to cut into small rectangles and circles.

2. Make 3 layers of pastry shapes for each petit four. Peel the fruit, cut the kiwis into thin circles, and cut the mangos in long, thin slices.

Passion Fruit Millefeuilles

3. Make the pastry cream using the ingredients listed above (see basic recipe), and divide into 3 different bowls. Flavor one with rum, the second with passion fruit liqueur, and leave the third as it is. Assemble the petits fours as explained in the text above.

4. Dust the plain petits fours with confectioners' sugar, ice the mango petits fours with warmed fondant, and glaze the kiwi petits fours with warmed mango jam.

Cherimoya

For the puff pastry:
(see basic recipe)
4 cups/500 g flour, sifted
1¾ cups/400 g butter
2 tsp/10 g salt
1¼ cups/300 ml water

To finish:
1 small jar cherimoya jam
3½ tbsp/50 g sugar
4 tsp/20 g ground cinnamon
1 egg, lightly beaten

Makes: 8–10 windmills
Preparation time: 30 minutes
Baking time: 20 minutes
Chilling time: 40 minutes
Difficulty: ★ ★

These pastries make an excellent centerpiece for a dinner party or for a child's birthday, as their whimsical shape will surprise and delight guests young and old. If the instructions for puff pastry are carefully followed, it is really quite easy to make, and the results will be tender, light and flaky. Lack of time, however, is no reason to avoid making this recipe, since frozen puff pastry can easily be bought. Alternatively, croissant pastry may be used, as it is faster to make.

This recipe is versatile enough to accomodate many different tastes. Here cherimoya jam was chosen to fill the windmills, but any other exotic flavor or jam may be substituted. For a more pronounced spice flavor, the cinnamon is dusted on top of the pastries, rather than blended into the dough. Other spices—for example, nutmeg—may be used if preferred. Granulated sugar, sprinkled on top before baking, will caramelize in the oven for a sweet crunchy finish.

This unique windmill shape is fun to make, and not difficult at all; however, those who wish to simplify the process can simply fold the pastry over once to make turnovers. In this case, the edges of the pastry squares must be generously brushed with beaten egg, then folded and tightly pinched all around to seal the sides of the turnover.

1. Make the puff pastry according to the basic recipe, but using the amounts above. When the rolling and folding process is complete, refrigerate the pastry for 20 minutes.

2. Roll the pastry into a large square approximately 8 x 8 in/20 x 20 cm and ⅛ in/3 mm thick. Then cut it into 4 smaller squares.

Windmill Pastries

3. Mix the sugar and cinnamon and dust the 4 squares of pastry with it. Make 4 diagonal cuts in each square, from each corner almost into the center.

4. Cover the entire surface of each square with a layer of jam. Fold each corner over to the next corner and pinch gently. Brush the surface with the lightly beaten egg, sprinkle with sugar and bake 20 minutes at 355 °F/180 °C. Watch closely during baking to avoid burning the sugar or pastry.

4 cups/500 g flour, sifted
⅜ oz/10 g fresh compressed yeast
4 tsp/20 g freshly ground cumin and
    several whole seeds
1¼ cups/300 ml water
2 tsp/10 g salt
1½ tbsp/20 g freshly ground pepper

Makes:	*10–12 rolls*
Preparation time:	*20 minutes*
Rising time:	*1 hour*
Baking time:	*20 minutes*
Difficulty:	*★*

Bread, the "staff of life," is a food of ancient, even prehistoric origin. The Roman satirist Juvenal commented that *panem et circenses* (bread and circuses) were all that was necessary to keep the people happy. Perhaps the French Revolution would not have occurred if Marie Antoinette, in her famous remark, had not suggested that the people eat cake instead! The warm fragrant spices in this bread will keep people very happy indeed.

This recipe follows tradition in that it is easy to make by hand. The rolls do not require an electric mixer or bread machine; rather, a wooden spoon and some elbow grease are all that is needed to make a light, airy dough.

First, the yeast should be mixed with a little water. Then the flour should be placed in a large mixing bowl, and a well made in the center. The cumin, water, and yeast are placed in the well, and the dough is mixed and kneaded for about 15 minutes. Then a hole is formed in the middle, the salt and ground pepper are added, and the dough is again kneaded for a few minutes. At this point the dough should be shaped into a ball, and left to rise for one hour at room temperature. After rising, the dough may be shaped into balls or ovals.

The secret to bread baking is moisture: A small ovenproof dish of water should be placed in the oven during baking, as the humidity gives the bread a rich golden amber color. The dough can also be brushed with water, which helps the ground cumin and pepper sprinkled on the rolls before baking stick.

These rolls look exotic and taste amazingly good.

1. Combine the flour, yeast and cumin in a large mixing bowl as described above. Add the water and knead for 15 minutes, by hand or with an electric mixer.

2. Add the salt and ground pepper and continue kneading the dough for 5 minutes.

Pepper Rolls

3. Turn the ball of dough onto a lightly floured work surface and continue kneading by hand. Shape into a ball, cover with a clean, dry cloth and let rise for 1 hour.

4. Divide the dough into 10–12 parts of equal size and shape into rolls. Slice across the top with a knife. Place the rolls on a greased baking sheet and sprinkle with cumin seeds and freshly ground pepper. Bake about 20 minutes at 430 °F/220 °C.

Cinnamon

1¼ cups/150 g white flour
1¼ cups/150 g finest whole wheat flour
1⅔ cups/200 g rye flour
2 tsp/10 g salt
1¼ cups/300 ml water
2½ tbsp/25 g yeast
5 tsp/25 g butter, softened
1 cup/150 g chopped walnuts
6 tbsp/80 g ground cinnamon

Serves	*6–8*
Preparation time:	*15 minutes*
Rising time:	*60 minutes*
Baking time:	*45 minutes*
Difficulty:	★

Bread is a traditional accompaniment to every meal, present on the table at every course in many cultures. Bread goes well with cheese, cold meats, or pasta dishes; just about everything. A hearty bread like this is practically a meal in itself and turns even the simplest accompaniments into a feast.

The best breads ideally have a wonderfully thick, crunchy crust and will keep for two or three days in a plastic bag. This recipe contains a higher proportion of rye flour than many, and thus tastes even better if it is allowed to rest, uncut, for a day or so after baking to develop its fullest flavor.

Properly sealed, fresh bread freezes very well. Individual slices may be then defrosted about 20 seconds on high power in the microwave, for a just-baked taste.

The top of this bread may be lightly dusted with flour before baking, to add to its natural look and texture. The walnuts should be chopped before they are added to the dough. They may be replaced with dark or golden raisins, chopped almonds or hazelnuts. Similarly, the bread may be made with olives or pine nuts, adjusting the spices to taste, for a savory addition to simple meals of fish or salad.

1. Combine the 3 types of flour, the salt and water. Knead or mix with an electric mixer until the dough is smooth and soft, not crumbly.

2. Mix the yeast in a bit of water, then add to the dough. Then blend in the softened butter. Knead the dough for 15 minutes until the dough is well blended and smooth.

Walnut Bread

3. Add the cinnamon and chopped walnuts and let the dough rise for 30 minutes.

4. Shape the dough into a ball and snip the top with scissors. Place the ball on a greased, floured baking sheet and let rise again for 30 minutes, until it doubles in size. Dust the top with flour and bake for 45 minutes at 430 °F/220 °C.

For the brioche dough:
4 cups/500 g flour, sifted
2 tsp/10 g salt
¼ cup/60 g sugar
3½ tbsp/50 ml water
¾ oz/20 g yeast
10 tbsp/150 g butter, softened
3 eggs

For the pastry cream:
  (see basic recipe)
4 vanilla beans
2 cups/500 ml milk

3 eggs
½ cup/125 g sugar
6½ tbsp/50 g cornstarch

To finish:
1 cup/150 g candied fruit
½ cup/50 g dark and golden raisins
3½ tbsp/50 ml dark rum
1 egg, lightly beaten

Makes:	20 rolls
Preparation time:	25 minutes
Rising time:	1 hour
Baking time:	15–20 minutes
Difficulty:	★

These sweet rolls give a mouthwatering twist to the familiar sticky cinnamon bun. Everyone will love these snail-shaped pastries, scented with the heady aroma of vanilla, luscious with cream, and sticky with raisins and candied fruit.

The flavor can be varied depending on which fruit juice or alcohol is used to soak the raisins and candied fruit, and a more intense vanilla flavor can be created by using Licor 43 or pure vanilla extract. The fruit must be drained thoroughly before it is added to the dough.

The choice of candied fruit to be added to the pastry cream is left up to you: The brighter the colors—red, yellow, green—the more appetizing the final result!

The surface of the rolls should be brushed with beaten egg before baking, to give them a shiny golden crust. They will keep well in the freezer, and so are very convenient to defrost whenever needed, for a winter dessert served with mint or jasmine tea, for breakfast with coffee, or on a sunny afternoon served with cold orange or grapefruit juice.

1. Soak the diced candied fruit and raisins in the rum. To make the dough, combine the flour, salt, sugar, water and eggs in a large mixing bowl. Beat thoroughly with an electric mixer, then add the yeast and softened butter.

2. Continue beating until the dough pulls away from the sides of the bowl. Set aside to rise for one hour at room temperature. Make the pastry cream (see basic recipe). Turn the dough onto a lightly floured surface and roll evenly to a thickness of ¼ in/5 mm. Using a long spatula, cover the whole surface of the dough with the cream.

Raisin Rolls

3. Drain the fruit and sprinkle evenly all over the pastry cream. Then roll the dough into a log.

4. Cut the log in slices about ¾ in/2 cm thick. Place on a greased or non-stick baking sheet. Brush the surface with the lightly beaten egg, and bake 15–20 minutes at 355 °F/180 °C.

Rum Raisin

1¼ cups/150 g flour, sifted
1¼ cups/150 g fine whole wheat flour
1⅔ cups/200 g rye flour
1¼ cups/300 ml water
a pinch of sugar
1 oz/25 g yeast

5 tsp/25 g butter, softened
2 tsp/10 g salt
generous ½ cup/100 g golden raisins
generous ½ cup/100 g dark raisins
¾ cup/200 ml dark rum
1 egg, lightly beaten

Makes:	4 braided loaves
Preparation time:	15 minutes
Rising time:	30 minutes
Baking time:	45 minutes
Difficulty:	★

Braided raisin bread is one of the most attractive breads around, with its pretty shape and suggestion of Rapunzel-like tresses. This is a bread dough that tastes better the longer it is kneaded, which should be at least 15 minutes. The dough should have a good springy texture for best results.

The raisins will have a more intense flavor if they have been soaked in the rum overnight, but if this is not possible, they may be soaked for one hour in boiling water, then one hour in the rum. The raisins and rum together enhance the naturally delicious yeast bread flavor. For a non-alcoholic version, the rum may be replaced with fruit juice used the same way.

The oven should be preheated for at least ten minutes so that the bread begins to bake as soon as it is put in the oven, which helps it to rise. A little moisture in the oven, achieved by placing a small dish of water in the oven during baking, yields a crisp crunchy crust with a soft inside.

This bread is delicious for breakfast with butter and jam, or served for lunch with a bountiful cheese plate or salad.

1. Soak the raisins in the rum, overnight if possible. To make the dough, combine the 3 types of flour in a large mixing bowl. Add the water and sugar, mix, then knead for 5 minutes.

2. Add the yeast and the butter in knobs; blend and knead for another 10 minutes. Add the salt towards the end.

Bread

3. Stir in the raisins and the rum and knead briefly. Then shape the dough into a ball, cover with a clean, dry cloth and set aside to rise for 30 minutes.

4. To make the braids, divide the dough into 3 strands per loaf and braid them. Place the braided loaves on a greased, floured baking sheet and let rise at room temperature until doubled in size. Glaze with the egg, then bake 45 minutes at 430 °F/220 °C.

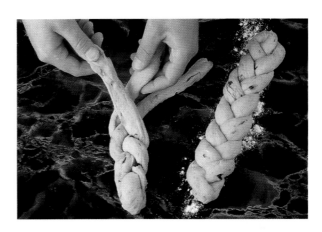

2 cups/250 g rye flour
2 cups/250 g white flour
1 tsp/5 g ground anise
1 tsp/5 g cinnamon
1 tsp/5 g coriander
4 cloves, ground
1 tsp/5 g nutmeg
⅜ oz/10 g yeast or 1 tbsp baking powder
grated rind of 1 orange
2 vanilla beans
6 eggs
1½ cups/500 g honey

For the pans:
4 tsp/20 g butter
8 tsp/20 g flour

To finish:
1 egg, lightly beaten

Makes: 25 small cakes
Preparation time: 20 minutes
Baking time: 15–20 minutes
Difficulty: ★

Gingerbread, or *pain d'epice* (spice bread) as it is called in French, has existed for many centuries. It may have been introduced to Europe by crusaders returning from the Middle East. In France, King Henry IV was a gingerbread fan, and the city of Reims was renowned for this specialty until the French Revolution. Nowadays the city of Dijon has that glorious reputation, and runs a flourishing trade in gingerbread.

The heavenly smell of gingerbread baking is enough to bring back long-forgotten memories of childhood in a single magical moment. This version of the traditional recipe was created by a Creole grandmother named Luz, who lives in Paris but yearns for the sunshine and light of her native islands. She has been making this gingerbread for years, to the great delight of all her children and grandchildren.

In her recipe, the grated orange rind and vanilla bring out all the other flavors; they are the essential elements. After the orange and vanilla, whatever spices are used are up to the cook.

Preparing the batter the day before and leaving it overnight in the refrigerator will make it easier to spoon out and give the flavors a chance to mingle and mellow, making the cake taste even better! Shaping the gingerbread is also part of the fun, and different molds or tartlet pans are perfect if available.

This recipe is filled with the taste of sunshine and nostalgia for the happy days of long ago.

1. Sift the 2 types of flour together in a large mixing bowl. Add the spices and yeast and stir briskly. Add the grated orange rind and the grainy insides of the vanilla bean. Blend well.

2. Add the eggs and honey, and mix thoroughly. The batter should be fairly thick; if it is left in the refrigerator overnight it will be solid enough to roll out and cut into shapes.

Gingerbread

3. Spoon the batter into buttered, floured tartlet pans.

4. Use a pastry brush to glaze the top of each cake with the lightly beaten egg. Bake 20 minutes at 320 °F/160 °C. Remove from the pans and cool on a rack.

Three-Cream

For the choux pastry:
(see basic recipe)
13 tbsp/200 g butter
2 cups/500 ml water
½ tsp sugar
½ tsp salt
2½ cups/300 g flour, sifted
7 eggs

For the pastry cream:
(see basic recipe)
4 vanilla beans
2 cups/500 ml milk
3 eggs
½ cup/125 g sugar
6½ tbsp/50 g cornstarch

3½ tbsp/50 ml dark rum
3½ tbsp/50 ml banana liqueur
3½ tbsp/50 ml passion fruit liqueur

For the caramel:
1 cup/250 g sugar
1 tbsp glucose syrup
2 tbsp water

To finish:
1 egg, lightly beaten
3½ oz/100 g fondant, melted
food coloring
1 tbsp/10 g chocolate sprinkles

Makes: 40–50 tiny cream puffs

Preparation time: 1 hour
Baking time: 20 minutes
Difficulty: ★ ★

Choux pastry, the classic cream puff dough, used to be called "hot dough" because it is cooked twice, first on the stove, then in the oven, to create its characteristic airy texture. It is simple to prepare as long as the instructions, elaborated in the basic recipe, are followed carefully. A half and half mixture of water and milk can be used instead of water for a richer pastry. Choux pastry is also used to make éclairs, as in the next recipe.

A pastry bag is the best means of shaping the dough into tiny balls or logs, which should be spaced well apart on the baking sheet. A pastry brush is used to glaze the tops with beaten egg for a shiny golden crust. The cream puffs should be baked until lightly browned, but the oven door must not be opened during baking. The door is first opened once the puffs are done, and they are then left in the oven to cool slowly; this prevents the cream puffs from "falling."

Caramel may be used to garnish the serving dish as well as to ice some of the cream puffs. It should be cooked until it just becomes light brown, then poured into a paper cone or pastry bag which can be used to squeeze decorative shapes onto an oiled baking sheet. When the caramel decorations have cooled, place them among the cream puffs around the serving plate for an elegant, edible finish. Another delectable possibility, beloved by ice cream fans, it to split the puffs and fill them with vanilla ice cream, then glaze the tops with melted chocolate.

1. Make the choux pastry according to the basic recipe, but using the amounts listed above.

2. Fill a pastry bag with the dough and squeeze small balls onto a non-stick baking sheet or parchment paper. Brush the tops with the lightly beaten egg. Make the pastry cream, again using the ingredients given above, and divide it among 3 different bowls. Flavor each bowl differently: one with rum, one with banana liqueur, and the last with passion fruit liqueur.

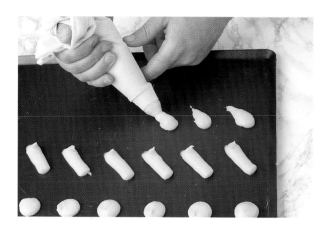

Profiteroles

3. Bake the cream puffs for 20 minutes at 320 °F/160 °C. When cooled, poke a hole in each and use a pastry bag to fill with the various pastry creams. Make the caramel by boiling the sugar, glucose syrup and water together until golden amber in color (about 320 °F/160 °C).

4. Dip the tops of some cream puffs in the caramel. Divide the melted fondant into 3 small bowls. Add a few drops of food coloring to each bowl, stir, then dip the remaining puffs in the fondant. Garnish with chocolate sprinkles.

Miniature Chocolate,

For the choux pastry:
(see basic recipe)
2 cups/500 ml water
13 tbsp/200 g butter
½ tsp sugar
½ tsp salt
2½ cups/300 g flour, sifted
7 eggs

For the pastry cream:
(see basic recipe)
4 vanilla beans
2 cups/500 ml milk
3 eggs
½ cup/125 g sugar
6½ tbsp/50 g cornstarch

the grated rind of 1 lime
½ cup/50 g unsweetened cocoa powder
⅔ cup/100 g green pistachios, finely
   chopped
a few drops coffee extract
a few drops vanilla extract

For the decoration:
4 oz/120 g fondant, melted

Makes:	*40 small éclairs*
Preparation time:	*40 minutes*
Baking time:	*20 minutes*
Difficulty:	★ ★

There are diverging opinions about the origin of the name *éclair,* which means lightning. Some people say that these pastries are quick as lightning both to make and to be eaten. Another version tells the tale of a mother, isolated by the snow in a remote mountain chalet, who had only a few eggs and some butter and flour left. She whipped up this invention in a flash to satisfy the hunger of her young ones. The recipe we know today still uses the simplest of ingredients to make an exceptionally light, airy pastry.

The fondant, divided among three different bowls, is especially nice when tinted with just a hint of natural colorings:

unsweetened cocoa powder in one, coffee extract in another, and vanilla extract in the third (a drop or two of yellow food coloring may be used to brighten the vanilla fondant). This sweet hard glaze adds just the right flavor and texture to balance the custardy cream filling.

To make the fondant shiny, it should be heated to body temperature, that is, about 98.6 °F/37 °C. This can be tested by touching a bit of the fondant to the lower lip; no difference in temperature should be felt.

Take your time to savor these marvelous little pastries, and try serving them with fresh, homemade lemonade.

1. Prepare the choux pastry and pastry cream according to the basic recipes but using the ingredients listed above. Fill a pastry bag with the choux pastry and squeeze log shapes onto a baking sheet. Bake 20 minutes at 320 °F/160 °C.

2. When the pastry cream has cooled, divide it into 3 bowls. Flavor one with the grated lime rind and half of the unsweetened cocoa powder; flavor the second with the finely chopped pistachios and coffee extract. Leave the third simply vanilla-flavored (as it is).

Vanilla, and Coffee Éclairs

3. Cut the éclairs in half lengthwise and fill them with the different flavored fillings.

4. Divide the melted fondant into 3 bowls. Add the remaining cocoa powder to one, a few drops of coffee extract to the second, and a few drops of vanilla extract to the third. Use a spatula to ice the top of each éclair with a complementary fondant.

Miniature Antilles

1 cup/100 g dark raisins
3½ tbsp/50 ml rum or juice
¾ oz/20 g yeast
6½ tbsp/100 ml milk
5 eggs
4 cups/500 g flour, sifted
2 tsp/10 g salt
3½ tbsp/50 g sugar
13 tbsp/200 g butter, softened

To finish:
confectioners' sugar
1 small jar papaya jam
1 small jar banana jam
1 small jar cherimoya jam

Makes: 15 small cakes
Preparation time: 20 minutes
Rising time: 30 minutes
Baking time: 30 minutes
Difficulty: ★ ★

Kugelhopf is a typically Alsatian cake, baked in a fluted ring pan and garnished with raisins. Myriad variations of it are also baked throughout Germany and Eastern Europe. In France it became fashionable under Queen Marie-Antoinette, who prized it for breakfast or afternoon tea. Perhaps this was the famous cake which she wished her people eat! On the first of April, to commemorate April Fools' Day (*poissons d'Avril*, or "April fish"), French bakers still follow the tradition of making their kugelhopf in a fish-shaped mold.

The brioche-type batter should be allowed to rise fully before baking, and like all leavened doughs, it needs to be thoroughly beaten and kneaded to develop a fine texture. The softened butter should not be added until the dough pulls away from the sides of the mixing bowl.

The raisins are added once the butter has been completely blended into the dough. After soaking, the raisins must be drained and patted dry, or they will wet the dough with excess liquid. Dried currants make an excellent subsitute for the raisins, if desired: They are seedless, full of vitamins, and have a similar sweet flavor.

A cross between bread and cake, these adorable little Kugelhopfs are perfect after-school snacks for children, while adults will enjoy them with a cup of tea.

1. Marinate the raisins in the rum until they expand. Meanwhile, start the dough by mixing the yeast in the milk. Break the eggs into the sifted flour.

2. Add the milk and yeast to the eggs and flour, mix well, then add the salt and sugar. Beat until the batter is smooth and well-blended.

Kugelhopf Cakes

3. Add the softened butter to the batter, blend thoroughly, then add the drained raisins and continue kneading.

4. Butter the miniature kugelhopf pans, fill each with batter, then set aside to rise at room temperature for 30 minutes. Preheat the oven, and bake for 30 minutes at 355 °F/180 °C. Remove the cakes from the pans, cool on a rack, then fill the centers with exotic jams. Dust with confectioners' sugar just before serving.

Grapefruit

For the croissant pastry:
4 cups/500 g flour
2 tsp/10 g salt
3½ tbsp/50 g sugar
2 cups/500 ml milk
grated rind of 1 grapefruit
1⅔ cups/400 g butter
⅜ oz/10 g fresh compressed yeast

For the filling:
1 lb/ 500 g dark chocolate

To finish:
1 egg, lightly beaten

Makes:	30 pastries
Preparation time:	30 minutes
Baking time:	20 minutes
Chilling time:	30 minutes
Difficulty:	★ ★

In the vast repertoire of French pastries, none is more fundamentally satisfying than *pains au chocolat*, or "chocolate breads." This variation was created by a French baker who understood that variety is the spice of life, and that people love to vary their snacks. For instance, the dough may be flavored with grated orange, lemon or lime rind instead of grapefruit.

These pastries are made with the same dough and technique as croissants, only shaped into long bands folded over and over to form a rectangle around a small bar of tasty dark chocolate. To cut the chocolate into neat bars, the knife blade should be heated between cuts. Alternatively, a few spoonfuls of good quality chocolate chips will work well. Other types of chocolate may be used, for example milk chocolate, or chocolate with almonds or hazelnuts.

If making croissant dough seems a bit intimidating or time-consuming, a simpler variation may be made using ordinary bread dough.

Pains au chocolats are delightful served warm or cold with hot chocolate or coffee, or with fruit juice on a hot sunny day.

1. In a large mixing bowl, combine the flour, salt, sugar, milk and the grated rind. Only when the dough is well blended, add the yeast and continue kneading. Turn the dough onto a lightly floured board and roll out evenly. Place the butter in the center of the dough and fold all 4 sides over the butter, then roll out again in a long rectangle.

2. Turn the dough 90 degrees, fold it in thirds toward the middle, and refrigerate briefly before rolling out again. Repeat this process (rolling into a rectangle, folding in thirds, and turning) 3 times. Refrigerate the dough for 30 minutes. Cut the chocolate; or melt and fill a pastry bag with it, and squeeze about 30 long thin bars of chocolate onto parchment paper. Let harden.

Pain au Chocolat

3. When the dough is finished, roll it out into squares and cut them into long bands about 2 in/5 cm wide.

4. Place a small bar of chocolate at one end of a band of pastry, fold over 3 times, then cut. Repeat the process to make about 30 pastries. Brush the tops with the lightly beaten egg, and bake about 20 minutes at 355 °F/180 °C.

Chocolate and Coffee

For the sugar cookie dough:
1 cup/250 g butter, softened
1 cup/250 g sugar
2 eggs
4 cups/500 g flour, sifted
½ tbsp/5 g baking powder

For the chocolate icing:
3½ oz/100 g tempered dark chocolate

For the coffee icing:
1 egg
2 tbsp instant coffee powder

To finish:
½ cup/50 g shredded coconut

Makes:	*40 cookies*
Preparation time:	*25 minutes*
Baking time:	*10–15 minutes*
Chilling time:	*15 minutes*
Difficulty:	★ ★

This particular kind of sugar cookie dough, called *pâte sablée* in French, calls for more butter than most doughs; this gives it its characteristic light, crisp, crumbly texture. This recipe uses equal parts butter and sugar to make them even lighter.

Half of the sugar cookies should be glazed with chocolate, and the other half with coffee. The main difference in baking the two types of cookie is that the chocolate ones are dipped into the melted chocolate after baking and cooling. However, the coffee glaze, made of beaten egg mixed with instant coffee, is brushed onto the surface of the cookies with a pastry brush before they are baked.

Try drawing decorative stripes on the surface of the dough with a fork before baking, or brush the unbaked cookies with egg and sprinkle with granulated brown sugar, which caramelizes in the oven. Diced dried fruit or chopped nuts, sprinkled on top of the egg glaze, are also flavorful garnishes.

These cookies are scrumptious served with cold milk, coffee or tea; the truly decadent may even wish to dunk them.

1. Cream the butter and sugar in a large mixing bowl until the sugar has completely dissolved in the butter.

2. Add the eggs and continue beating. Sift together the flour and baking powder, then add to the dough. Beat until the dough is soft and smooth. Refrigerate about 15 minutes.

Glazed Sugar Cookies

3. Roll out the cookie dough and cut shapes with cookie cutters; scalloped circles 2½ in/6–7 cm in diameter are traditional. Melt the chocolate in a double boiler until it reaches about 85 °F/30 °C. Mix the instant coffee powder with the lightly beaten egg until it dissolves.

4. Place the cookies on a non-stick baking sheet. Using a pastry brush, glaze half of them with the coffee-egg mixture. Bake 10–15 minutes at 355 °F/180 °C. Cool on a rack. Dip the tops of the plain cookies in the melted chocolate, and turn right side up to set.

Lime Meringue

For the short pastry:
(see basic recipe)
⅓ cup/50 g confectioners' sugar
1 egg
2 tbsp water
a pinch of salt
½ cup/125 g cold butter
the contents of 1 vanilla bean
2 cups/250 g flour, sifted

For the lime filling:
¾ cup/200 ml lime juice or
   the juice of 3 limes
6½ tbsp/100 g butter
¾ cup plus 1 tbsp/200 g sugar, divided
3 eggs
⅓ cup/40 g cornstarch

Makes: 30 tartlets
Preparation time: 30 minutes
Baking time: 15 minutes
Difficulty: ★ ★

For the meringue:
5 egg whites
a pinch of salt
1 cup/250 g sugar
3½ tbsp/50 ml water

Lemons and limes have been used for centuries, for both culinary and medicinal purposes. They originally came from India, were known to the Persians and highly esteemed by the Greeks, and came to Europe with crusaders returning from Palestine.

Though lemon meringue is more traditional, limes are used in this recipe for a change, but any citrus fruit works well. The finely grated rind may be added to the short pastry to heighten the flavor. Refrigerating the pastry for one or two hours before rolling it out will make it easier to handle.

The tarts are topped with Italian meringue, made with hot sugar syrup, which is more compact and foamier but smoother than plain beaten egg whites, and thus more suitable for decorating. A chef's trick is to add a pinch of sugar or salt while beating the whites to prevent them from becoming grainy. Meringue usually has a pristine white color, but if it strikes your fancy, a drop or two of food coloring may be added.

The meringue-covered tartlets need to be watched closely in the oven, as meringue browns and can burn very quickly, which would be an unfortunate outcome after all your hard work. The tartlets are easiest to make if the steps are organized like an assembly line: first bake, then fill, then top with meringue.

These delectable little pastries are a study in perfectly balanced contrast: the rich firm dough encloses a smooth tangy filling, topped with a sweet cloud of fluffy meringue. Mmmmmmmm....

1. Make the short pastry (see basic recipe). Line the tartlet pans with pastry, weight the dough with beads or dried beans, and bake 15 minutes at 340 °F/170 °C. For the filling, whisk together the lime juice, butter, and 1 tbsp sugar and bring to a boil. In a separate bowl, beat the eggs with the remaining sugar and cornstarch. Add to the boiling mixture.

2. Let the mixture cook, stirring constantly until it thickens. Then remove from the heat and continue stirring until it has completely cooled. Fill the tartlet shells with the lime mixture.

Tartlets

3. In a large mixing bowl, beat the egg whites and salt until stiff. Cook the sugar and the water in a heavy bottomed pot until it reaches 250 °F/120 °C. Then pour this sugar syrup in a thin stream into the egg whites, beating continuously until the mixture has cooled.

4. Use a pastry bag to pipe the meringue onto the tartlets. Place under the broiler for a few moments until the meringue begins to brown slightly. Serve immediately on an elegant plate.

For the puff pastry:
(see basic recipe)
2 cups/250 g flour, sifted
13 tbsp/200 g butter
1 tsp/5 g salt
⅔ cup/150 ml water
3½ tbsp/50 g sugar

To finish:
1¾ oz/50 g fondant
a few drops coffee extract

Makes: 40–50 pastries
Preparation time: 20 minutes
Baking time: 15–20 minutes
Difficulty: ★

Puff pastry, called *pâte feuillété* in French, was created in the 17th century. Some attribute its origin to the pastry chef Sire Feuillet, who worked for a high official at the time. But the painter Le Lorrain, a pastry chef by trade, claims he invented it while experimenting in his kitchen. There are yet more legends about its origin, none of which can be proven, but one thing is certain: This airy, buttery pastry was not widely known until the 19th century, when the standard five repetitions of the folding process became established as the definitive technique.

Puff pastry can only succeed if the rule of five is followed, creating multiple alternating layers of pastry and butter. The heat of the oven evaporates the moisture in the dough, causing the layers to swell up, held back only by the flour and butter content. The result is an airy, puffy, fragile pastry that melts in the mouth with the heavenly taste of butter. The butter should be of the best quality—do not substitute margarine!—and the baking must be monitored carefully so the pastry does not burn.

Some tasty variations could include a hint of vanilla extract or cocoa powder added to the melted fondant.

These little palm hearts are easy to make; to save time, they may even be made with store-bought, frozen puff pastry.

1. Make the puff pastry according to the basic recipe, using the ingredients listed above except the sugar. Roll out the pastry in a large circle on a lightly floured surface. Dust the circle with some of the sugar and continue rolling it out.

2. Roll two edges of the circle towards each other in the center, forming tight parallel spirals.

Palm Pastries

3. Cut the double roll of pastry into slices about ½ in/1.5 cm thick. Heat the fondant slightly and add the coffee extract.

4. Sprinkle some sugar on each slice, then flatten slightly with a rolling pin to make the characteristic palm heart shape. Place on a non-stick baking sheet and bake 15–20 minutes at 355 °F/180 °C. When the pastries have cooled, decorate with the fondant and serve.

Glossary

ALMOND FLOUR: Blanched almonds which have been ground to a powder. Almond flour is sold commercially or can be made by chopping blanched almonds in a food processor until they have a powdery consistency.

APRICOT GLAZE: Hot, strained apricot jam can be spread onto pastries, either as a glaze or as an isolating layer between cake and moist cream or fruit fillings.

BAIN-MARIE: Also called water bath, a gentle method of heating used to either cook food or keep food warm, a bain-marie consists of a pan containing food placed inside a larger pan of warm (not boiling) water, surrounding the smaller pan with heat. Placed in an oven, a bain-marie generates steam for foods that require moister heat than that generated by home ovens.

BISCUIT: The French word for sponge cake.

TO BLANCH: Briefly immersing foods in boiling water and then immediately in cold water to stop the cooking. This process makes it easier to remove peels and skins, rids food of impurities, and preserves the flavor and color of food before freezing.

BLINI PAN: A small cast iron pan approximately 5 in/13 cm in diameter with a thick bottom and high sides which is used to make blinis. Blini pans are also used to caramelize the tops of custards by heating the pan and placing it directly on a sugared surface.

BLINIS OR BLINTZES: Small savory pancakes made with white and buckwheat flour and leavened with yeast.

BRICK PASTRY: see *Feuille de brick.*

BRIOCHE: A classic French yeast bread, very light, yet made rich by eggs and butter.

CARAMEL: Caramel is produced when sugar is heated to 320-350 °F/160-177 °C and becomes light to dark brown. Other ingredients like water, cream and butter are added to the caramel to make sauces or candies, but liquid must be added carefully and gradually to sugar heated to these temperatures!

TO CARAMELIZE: To heat sugar until it becomes caramel (see above); or to coat something with caramel syrup; or to sprinkle sugar on the surface of a dessert and then broil or grill it briefly until the sugar turns into caramel (for example, a crème brûlée).

CHANTILLY: A term from French culinary vocabulary, *à la chantilly* means that a dish, sweet or savory, is served with or incorporates whipped cream. Crème chantilly is simply whipped cream, most often lightly sweetened with vanilla, sugar or liqueurs.

CHOUX PASTRY: A simple but unique dough that is prepared on the stovetop by bringing water or milk to a boil, adding flour and then stirring in several eggs to form a sticky paste. This is the classic cream puff pastry.

CLARIFIED BUTTER: Butter that has been melted slowly without stirring, then skimmed and decanted, leaving the milk solids and water in the pan. This liquid is pure butter fat and has a higher smoking point than whole butter, but less intense buttery flavor.

TO CLARIFY: To remove any particles which interfere with the clear appearance of liquids (i.e. jelly or consommé), usually by straining or binding the impurities, often by adding and then straining out egg white.

TO COAT: In baking, coating refers to covering the surface of cakes and pastries with a thin layer often of chocolate or marzipan.

CONFECTIONERS' SUGAR: American term for icing sugar, also known as powdered sugar.

COULIS: A thick sauce consisting primarily of puréed fruit, occasionally with lemon juice, sugar or other ingredients added to enhance its flavor.

CRÈME FRAÎCHE: A thickened cream with an incomparably smooth texture and nutty, not sour, taste. If not readily available, crème fraîche can be simulated by adding 1 tsp–1 tbsp buttermilk to 1 cup heavy cream and letting the mixture stand at room temperature 8–24 hours until thickened. This will keep up to 10 days in the refrigerator.

TO DEGLAZE: To use a liquid such as water, fruit juice, alcohol or stock to dissolve food particles remaining in a pan after food has been sautéed in it. This liquid is normally used as the basis of a sauce.

TO DICE: To cut fruit or vegetables into even, dice-like shapes. Traditionally, dice is about ¼–½ in/5 mm in size.

DOUBLE BOILER: A double boiler consists of two pans that nestle into each other. The bottom pan is filled with simmering water and the top pan rests over, but not in, the hot water, providing the gentle heat necessary to melt or cook delicate foods like custards or sauces. Compare to bain-marie.

FEUILLE DE BRICK: A paper-thin crêpe made with boiled semolina flour. Feuille de brick are made by spreading a thin layer of semolina dough onto a hot griddle and removing it almost immediately, before it browns. Feuille de brick are used for crispy outer casings of desserts in place of phyllo dough or puff pastry.

FEUILLETÉ: A French word meaning "flaky" and often used to refer to pastries which are made with rich, many-layered puff pastry. See also *Millefeuille.*

TO FLAMBÉ: To pour alcohol over food and light the alcohol, imparting a very special flavor. This can be a dramatic presentation or an earlier step in the cooking process.

TO FLOUR: Also called dusting, this means coating a greased baking pan with a very fine layer of flour so that the item baked in it can be more easily removed. Other ingredients can be used instead of flour including, for example, sugar, bread crumbs, sesame seeds, or finely ground almonds.

TO FOLD: Also to blend; a means of combining two mixtures of varying densities (for example, egg whites and custard). With the lighter mass on top of the heavier one, use a spatula to cut through both, scrape along the bottom of the bowl, and up the side. Continue this, rotating the bowl slightly with each stroke. Folding must be done carefully, gently, and yet rapidly to retain the volume of the lighter mixture.

FRANGIPANE: A variation of pastry cream that is usually flavored with ground almonds and used in various cakes and pastries.

FROMAGE BLANC: A mild fresh cheese similar to cottage cheese in flavor, but not in texture. Fromage blanc has a silky, smooth texture like that of sour cream.

GANACHE: An extraordinary, rich chocolate cream made by heating whipping cream and allowing chocolate to melt in it. Depending on its texture, ganache can be used as a coating, filling, or sauce.

TO GARNISH: Decorating a dish to make it more visually appealing with various edible elements; also refers to the decoration itself. Garnish varies from a single sprig of mint, to the additions to a soup, to entire side dishes.

GELATIN: A clear and flavorless substance used to jell liquid mixtures. Gelatin is available in ¼ oz/7 g envelopes of granules (more common in North America) and in paper-thin sheets or leaves (standard in Europe). Leaf gelatin should be soaked in cold water for 5–10 minutes, then thoroughly wrung out before, like ground gelatin, being dissolved in a small amount of hot liquid before use. One envelope of granules or 4 leaves of gelatin is generally sufficient to jell 2 cups/500 ml liquid.

GÉNOISE: A variation of sponge cake, in which whole eggs are beaten with sugar to the ribbon stage (see ribbon stage) before flour, finely-ground nuts, or other ingredients are folded in.

GLACÉ: A French term meaning chilled, iced or frozen.

TO GLAZE: To spread a thin layer of eggs, jelly or jam, gum arabic, or any other kind of coating onto foods to give them a shiny finish.

TO GREASE OR BUTTER: Brushing a thin layer of butter or some other fat onto baking pans so that the finished product can be removed from the pans without tearing.

HEAVY CREAM: This is the American term for double cream.

HOT OVEN: 400–425 °F or 205–220 °C

TO INFUSE: see to steep

INSTANT CUSTARD MIX: Unsweetened instant custard mix, also called *"poudre à flan."* Bird's English Custard Mix is one brand available on the market.

ITALIAN MERINGUE: A variation of meringue made by pouring hot sugar syrup over whipped egg whites while beating continuously until the mixture has cooled completely.

TO KNEAD: To thoroughly combine and work the components of a dough either by hand or with the dough hook of an electric mixer to produce a homogenous dough. It can take 15 minutes or longer to produce a smooth, elastic dough when kneading by hand.

LIGHT CREAM: This is the American term for single cream.

TO LINE: To cover the inside of a mold or pan with whatever ingredient is called for. For a charlotte, ladyfingers would be used. For aspic, the mold would be lined with gelatin.

LOW OVEN: 300–325 °F or 150–165 °C

TO MACERATE/MARINATE: To soak foods in an aromatic liquid (marinade) for a period of time to allow the food to take on the flavor of the liquid and become more tender. Fruits soaked in liqueur are macerated; meat or fish in a savory liquid is marinated.

MELON BALLER: A special spoon shaped like a tiny bowl used to carve circles from melons and other fruits and vegetables.

MERINGUE: A light mass of stiffly beaten egg whites, often sweetened with sugar, which can be used as an icing or topping, an element of a mousse, cream or soufflé, or baked as cookies or bases for gâteaux. See also Italian meringue.

MILLEFEUILLE: The French word literally means "thousand leaves" and refers to the multitude of buttery-light layers in perfect puff pastry. Mille-feuille is also a 3-tiered sweet consisting of puff pastry filled with cream, custard or fruit and dusted with confectioners' sugar or glazed on top. The classic version, with pastry cream, is known as a Napoleon in North America, or vanilla slice in Britain.

MODERATE OVEN: 350–375 °F or 175–190 °C

PÂTE: The French word for many kinds of mixtures in baking, including dough, batter and pastry. Short pastry is *pâte brisée*, short sweet pastry is *pâte sucrée*, crêpe batter is *pâte à crêpe*, and so forth.

TO POACH: A method of cooking food by immersing it in hot, but not boiling, water or other liquid.

TO PREBAKE: To bake a pie crust or pastry shell without a filling. Prick the pastry with fork and weight it down with dried beans or baking beans so it does not rise or contort while baking.

TO PURÉE: To blend or mash food until it has a perfectly smooth consistency, often by means of a blender or food processor. Purée also refers to the puréed food itself.

QUENELLE: An oval-shaped scoop of mousse, ice cream or any other unctuous ingredient shaped using two soup spoons.

TO RECONSTITUTE: To add liquid to dried or dehydrated foods, such as powdered milk or dried fruits and vegetables.

TO REFRESH: A means of preventing foods from continuing to cook in their own heat either by immersing the cooking pan in cold water or running cold water directly onto the food immediately after removing it from the heat.

RIBBON STAGE: When beating sugar with eggs, they should become pale yellow and reach the ribbon stage, so called because the mixture falls in silky ribbons from the whisk or beaters.

SABAYON: Also known by its Italian name, zabaglione, it is an extremely light, frothy custard consisting of egg yolks, sugar and wine or other spirits that are vigorously whisked over a gentle source of heat.

TO SAUTÉ: A method of cooking in a very small amount of hot oil or other fat, usually in an uncovered pan. Food may be lightly sautéed just to brown its surface, or cooked all the way through.

SPONGE CAKE: A classic sponge cake consists of egg whites and egg yolks, each beaten separately with sugar until light and foamy, then folded together and enriched with a little flour, ground nuts, or other ingredients. There are virtually infinite variations of sponge cakes, and they form the basis of a vast array of gâteaux and other desserts.

SPUN SUGAR: Thin filaments of cooked or caramelized sugar which are "spun" by drawing them across a flat, clean surface. Spun sugar can be gathered up to make nests, garlands or other decorations for desserts.

TO STEEP OR INFUSE: To soak an ingredient in a liquid, usually hot, for several minutes in order to impart its flavor to the liquid (for example, tea in hot water, or a vanilla bean in milk when making custard).

TO STRAIN: To pour or press ingredients through a sieve or a piece of cheesecloth in order to remove impurities, lumps, or seeds.

SUGAR SYRUP: A solution of sugar and water that have been boiled together. It is indispensable in baking and confection-making. The density of sugar syrup varies according to the proportions of sugar and water used; unless otherwise noted the recipes in this volume call for a heavy syrup made of equal parts sugar and water.

TO TEMPER: A method of preparing chocolate to be used for decorative work or coating by slowly melting it, then allowing it to partially cool, then reheating it very briefly. This complex process serves to prevent the cocoa butter contained in the chocolate from crystallizing, which would severely detract from the appearance of the finished product.

TUILE: Literally meaning "tile" in French, a tuile is a very thin wafer that is draped over an object or placed in a form while still warm and flexible, resulting in decorative cookies that can also be used as vessels for custard, mousse, etc.

VANILLA SUGAR: Sugar infused with the flavor of vanilla bean, or containing some ground vanilla. This can easily be made at home by placing one or more vanilla beans in a jar filled with sugar. After a week or two the sugar will be permeated with the aroma of vanilla.

VERY HOT OVEN: 450–475 °F or 230–245 °C

Basic Recipes

Pastry Cream

Ingredients:
1 vanilla bean – 4 cups/1 liter milk, divided – 6 egg yolks – ¾ cup plus 1 tbsp/200 g sugar – 1 cup/120 g flour – 3½ tbsp/25 g cornstarch

Preparation:
Split the vanilla bean lengthwise and add it to 3⅔ cups/900 ml milk with the salt. Bring to a boil for 2 minutes, then remove from heat. Beat the yolks and sugar in a large mixing bowl until light and fluffy. Mix in the flour and the cornstarch, then the remaining cool milk. Add the hot milk and stir. Return to a boil for 3 minutes, whisking constantly. Allow to cool, then refrigerate.

Custard

Ingredients:
4 cups/1 liter milk – ¾ cup plus 1 tbsp/200 g sugar – 12 egg yolks

Preparation:
Bring the milk and half the sugar to a boil in a heavy-bottomed pot. Beat the eggs and remaining sugar in a mixing bowl. Stir a little hot milk into the egg mixture, then return to the pot of milk, stirring constantly with a wooden spoon. Do not allow to boil! Remove from the heat and stir constantly until cool. Strain through a sieve and refrigerate until needed.

Vanilla Custard

Ingredients:
1 vanilla bean – 1 cup/250 ml milk – 3 egg yolks – 3½ tbsp/50 g superfine sugar

Preparation:
Open the vanilla bean lengthwise and scrape the grainy insides into the milk; bring to a boil. Beat the egg yolks and sugar until fluffy and falling in a ribbon off the back of a spoon. Stirring constantly, pour the hot milk into the eggs and sugar, whisk and heat to 177 °F/80 °C. Remove from heat and transfer into a cool bowl. Refrigerate until needed.

Ladyfingers

Ingredients:
8 eggs, separated – 1 cup/250 g sugar, divided – 1½ cups plus 2 tbsp/190 g flour, sifted – ¾ tsp baking powder

Preparation:
Beat the egg yolks with 6½ tbsp/100 g sugar to the ribbon stage. In a clean bowl, beat the egg whites with the remaining sugar until stiff. Fold the meringue into the yolks and sugar. Sift the flour and baking powder together and fold into the egg mixture. Pipe finger shapes onto a baking sheet and bake at 390 °F/200 °C for 10–15 minutes.

Biscuit

Ingredients:
6 large eggs – 1 cup/250 g sugar – 3 tsp warm water – 2 cups/250 g flour, sifted – a pinch of salt

Preparation:
Combine the eggs and sugar in a large mixing bowl, beating with an electric mixer until the batter falls in a ribbon off the beater and is pale yellow. Stir in the water, then flour and salt until well blended. Bake at 390 °F/200 °C for 10–15 minutes.

Génoise

Ingredients:
4 eggs – ½ cup/125 g sugar – 1 cup/125 g flour, sifted

Preparation:
Beat the eggs and sugar together in a large mixing bowl until light and fluffy. Place the bowl over a double boiler and whisk constantly until the mixture doubles in volume. Remove from heat. Whisk until completely cooled, then mix in the sifted flour bit by bit. Bake 20 minutes at 355 °F/180 °C.

Dacquoise

Ingredients:
5 oz/150 g whites (white of 5 large eggs) – ¾ cup/175 g sugar, divided – ¼ cup/50 g finely ground almonds – (1⅔ cups/150 g shredded coconut for coconut dacquoise)

Preparation:
Beat the egg whites with 3½ tbsp/50 g sugar until stiff, then fold in the finely ground almonds and the rest of the sugar (and the shredded coconut for coconut dacquoise). Fill a pastry bag with the mixture and squeeze onto a baking sheet lined with baking parchment. Bake 30 minutes at 340 °F/170 °C.

Crêpe Batter

Ingredients:
2 cups/250 g flour, sifted – 6 eggs – 2 cups/500 ml milk – 1 cup/250 ml heavy cream – a few drops Grand Marnier – a few drops vanilla extract – ¼ cup/60 g butter

Preparation:
Sift the flour into a large mixing bowl. Make a well in the center and whisk in the eggs one by one. Gradually add the milk, cream, Grand Marnier and vanilla extract, whisking well to avoid any lumps. Brown the butter in a frying pan, then mix into the batter. Let the batter rest before making the crêpes.

Basic Recipes

Choux Pastry

Ingredients:
1 cup/250 ml milk – 1 tsp/5 g salt – 1 tsp/5 g sugar – 6½ tbsp/100 g butter, cut into small pieces – 1¼ cups/150 g flour, sifted

Preparation:
Combine the milk, salt, sugar, and butter in a large pot and bring to a boil. As soon as the butter melts, add the flour and stir briskly with a wooden spoon until well blended. Reduce heat to low and stir constantly for 10 minutes until the batter pulls away from the sides of the pot and pulls off the spoon. Remove from heat, then add the eggs one by one, stirring well each time. The batter should not be too runny or too stiff. Bake according to the recipe.

Rich Tart Pastry

Ingredients:
1⅔ cups/200 g flour, sifted – ⅔ cup/100 g confectioners' sugar – a pinch of salt – 6½ tbsp/100 g butter, cut in small pieces – 5 tbsp water or milk

Preparation:
Make a well with the flour, sugar and salt. Place the cold, cut butter in it and mix with the fingertips, adding the water or milk bit by bit. Then knead the dough with your palms, shape into a ball and refrigerate for 30 minutes. Blind bake at 390 °F/200 °C, twice for 10 minutes each time.

Short Pastry

Ingredients:
scant ¼ cup/30 g confectioners' sugar – 1 egg yolk – a pinch of salt – ¼ cup/60 g chilled butter – the contents of 1 vanilla bean – ¾ cup/90 g flour, sifted

Preparation:
Combine all the ingredients except the flour into a dough. Then add the flour little by little until well blended. Wrap the pastry in a clean dry cloth and refrigerate overnight. Press into a pie or tart pan. Prebake at 390 °F/200 °C, twice for 10 minutes each time.

Doughnuts

Ingredients:
1⅔ cups/200 g flour, sifted – 2 whole eggs – 1 tsp/5 g salt – 1½ tbsp/20 ml beer – 2½ tbsp/40 ml oil – 3 egg whites – oil for deep frying

Preparation:
Place the flour in a large mixing bowl. Make a well in the center and put the egg yolks, salt, and beer into the hole. Stir with a wooden spoon, blending in the flour little by little. Coat the surface with the oil to prevent a crust from forming on the dough while it rests. When ready to proceed, mix in the oil before shaping and deep-frying the doughnuts.

Eggwhite Pastry

Ingredients:
5 tbsp/75 g butter – ¼ cup/60 g sugar – the grated rind and juice of 1 lemon – ⅔ cups/75 g finely ground almonds – 1¼ cups/150 g flour, sifted – a pinch of salt – 3 egg whites

Preparation:
Cream the butter and sugar. Add the lemon rind and juice, almonds, flour and salt. Separately, beat the egg whites until stiff, then fold gently into the dough. Set aside for 30 minutes. Prebake at 390 °F/200 °C, twice for 10 minutes each time.

Puff Pastry

Ingredients:
generous 4½ cups/550 g flour, sifted –1½ tsp/8 g salt – 1 cup/250 ml water – 1½ cups plus 1 tbsp/375 g butter

Preparation:
Place the flour in a mound on a work surface and make a well in the middle. Place the salt and water in the well and mix the dough just until it holds together in a ball. Do not handle it more than necessary. Refrigerate for 20 minutes, then roll the dough into a large square. Place the softened but cold butter in the center and fold the 4 sides of pastry over the butter towards the center. Roll out again into a long rectangle and fold in overlapping thirds. Refrigerate for 20 minutes. Repeat this folding, rolling, and chilling process 6 times, giving the dough a quarter turn between each roll. Bake for 5 minutes at 430 °F/220 °C, then for 20 minutes at 390 °F/200 °C.

Butter Short Pastry

Ingredients:
½ cup/125 g butter, softened – 2 cups/250 g flour – 1 egg – 2 tsp water ⅓ cup/50 g confectioners' sugar – a pinch of salt – 1 vanilla bean

Preparation:
Cut the butter in small pieces into the flour. Blend with a pastry blender or fork. Add the egg, water, sugar and salt. Do not handle the dough more than necessary to blend the ingredients. Set aside for 30 minutes. Prebake at 390 °F/200 °C, twice for 10 minutes each time.

Sweet Short Pastry

Ingredients:
½ cup/125 g butter, softened – ½ cup/125 g sugar – 2 eggs – 2 cups/250 g flour, sifted – a pinch of salt

Preparation:
Cream the butter, sugar and eggs until fluffy. Then add the flour and salt. Knead by hand until the pastry is well blended. Refrigerate overnight, if possible, then press into a pie pan. Prebake at 390 °F/200 °C, twice for 10 minutes each time.

Basic Recipes

Brioche Dough

Ingredients:
⅜ oz/10 g compressed fresh yeast* – 4 generous cups/500 g flour, sifted – 2 tbsp/30 g sugar – 2 tsp/10 g salt – 1½ cups plus 1 tbsp/375 g butter – 8 eggs

Preparation:
Dissolve the yeast in a little warm water, then mix in ¾ cup plus 1 tbsp/100 g of the flour. Let rise in a warm place until doubled in volume. Make a well in the remaining flour. Put the sugar, salt, butter and 3 eggs in the well, combine to form a dough, and knead. Stir in the remaining 5 eggs one at a time, by hand. Add the yeast starter. Let the dough rise for 4 hours, then turn, punch down, and place in a baking pan. Again leave it to rise for 2 hours, then bake at 355 °F/180 °C until golden brown.

*In hot climates or where only active dry yeast is available, substitute half as much active dry yeast for the compressed fresh yeast.

Slightly Risen Pastry

Ingredients:
3 tsp/15 g compressed fresh yeast* – ½ cup/125 ml warm milk – ¼ cup plus 1 tsp/65 g butter; half melted, half softened – 2 cups/250 g flour, sifted – ½ cup/70 g confectioners' sugar – a pinch of salt – 1 tsp grated orange rind – 1 egg yolk

Preparation:
Combine the yeast and the warm milk, then add the melted butter. Pour this mixture over the flour and stir. Beat the sugar with the softened butter, salt and grated orange rind. Add to the flour mixture, combine to form a dough, and knead. Set aside to rise until doubled in volume. Bake for 40 minutes at 355 °F/180 °C.

*In hot climates or where only active dry yeast is available, substitute half as much active dry yeast for the compressed fresh yeast.

Praliné/Nut Brittle

Ingredients:
1 cup sugar – 6 tbsp water – 1 cup almonds or hazelnuts, toasted

Preparation:
Combine the sugar and water in large heavy pot. Cook until the sugar dissolves, then boil until it turns light caramel color (about 300 °F/150 °C). Add the nuts. Stir and cook until the caramel darkens (335 °F/168 °C), then pour onto an oiled baking sheet. Spread evenly and set aside until cool and hard. Break into chunks. Store in an airtight container until needed, then grind to desired consistency in a food processor. Caution: overprocessing creates praliné paste.

Vanilla Ice Cream

Ingredients:
4 cups/1 liter milk – ¾ cup plus 1 tbsp/200 g sugar, divided – 10 vanilla beans – 12 egg yolks – ½ cup/125 ml heavy cream

Preparation:
Boil the milk with half the sugar and the vanilla bean. Beat the egg yolks with the remaining sugar until light and fluffy. Pour some of the boiled milk into the eggs and sugar, mix, then pour all of the egg mixture into the hot milk. Stir and cook slowly until thickened. Add the cream, blend well, then process in an ice cream machine according to the manufacturer's instructions.

Whipped Cream

Ingredients:
2 cups/500 ml heavy cream, well chilled – 1⅓ cups/200 g confectioners' sugar – 1 tsp vanilla extract

Preparation:
Whisk the cold cream until it begins to thicken, then add the sugar and vanilla and continue beating until stiff. Be careful not to overbeat, or it will curdle into butter.

Fondant

Ingredients:
3 cups sugar – 1 cup water – ½ tbsp glucose syrup OR a pinch of cream of tartar

Preparation:
Combine the sugar and water in a large heavy pot. Cook slowly until the sugar is completely dissolved, stirring constantly. Stop stirring and bring just to a boil. Add the glucose or cream of tartar. Boil, without stirring, to soft ball consistency (238 °F/112 °C). Remove from heat and let stand for several minutes, then turn the mass onto a cool work surface. Let it cool to lukewarm, then beat with wooden spoon or paddle until white and firm. Knead by hand until smooth and creamy. Cover the fondant with a damp cloth and let rest at least 1 hour, then knead again to a glossy smooth texture. Refrigerate in an airtight container.

Sugar Syrup

Ingredients:
2½ cups/600 g white or 3 cups/600 g brown sugar – 4 cups/1 liter water

Preparation:
Dissolve the sugar in the water in a large heavy-bottomed pot. Bring to a boil and cook 3 more minutes. Remove from heat.

Index of Recipes